"In our urbanised world, what does it mean to live well in today's cities, where social and economic divides are an increasing reality? After many years of working in Kibera, Colin Smith brings us fresh and challenging insights through his study of the book of Luke. He brings this gospel into conversation with his life experiences in Nairobi so that we can begin to identify and navigate not only the gaps of wealth and poverty in the city, but also in our own lives. Through telling stories from his life and from others' lives, this book enables us to reflect on what transformation might look like both without and within."

Dr. Cathy Ross
Tutor at Church Mission Society and Ripon College Cuddesdon, Oxford, England

"There are few who with the quiet integrity of Colin Smith, with his decade working in the slums of Nairobi, can pen the conflicts involved in intentionally moving from wealth to be among the burgeoning urban poor. His extensive urban theological voice here produces a significant introduction to a lifestyle of engagement for all who would put on the dusty sandals of the master."

Viv Grigg, Chair, Encarnacao Alliance of Slum Movement Leaders and Professor of Urban Missiology at Azusa Pacific University, Azusa, California, United States

"Having worked with Colin in the Kibera Informal Settlement between 2004 and 2007, it became apparent to me as the vicar of St. Jerome Parish that he had a calling to serve among the poor and the marginalized in urban Africa. His ministry left a long-lasting impression on many in Africa. I was initiated into urban ministry through Colin's mentoring and encouragement. The issues in this book accurately reflect ministry practice in urban Africa. I encourage readers to pay close attention and put these principles into practice."

Richard Mayabi, General Secretary, Church Army Africa, Kibera Informal Settlement, Kenya

"Colin Smith writes prophetically, issuing a call to the people of Jesus to reimagine their ministry and witness at this time. In *Mind the Gap*, we are taken through a creative reengagement with Luke's Gospel in a way that opens it afresh to us and invites us into a different way of being a follower of Christ.

Colin is uniquely positioned to take us on this journey, and I think *Mind the Gap* should be read by all those concerned by the growing inequality in this world. In fact, it should be read by all those interested in what it means to walk in Christ's way in these times."

Craig Stewart, Director of The Warehouse, Cape Town, South Africa

Mind the Gap

Reflections from Luke's Gospel on the Divided City

Colin Smith

Series Editors

Kendi Howells Douglas
Stephen Burris

Urban Loft Publishers | Portland, Oregon

Urban Loft Publishers
2034 NE 40th Avenue #414
Portland, OR 97212
www.urbanloftpublishers.com

ISBN-13: 978-0692491744

Made in the U.S.A

Table of Contents

Series Preface / 7
Dedication / 9
Preface / 11
Introduction / 13

Chapter 1: Approaching the City 21
Chapter 2: Behind the Scenes: Luke's Context and Ours 31
Chapter 3: A World of Us and Them 41
Chapter 4: Making Some Early Connections: Luke's Context and Ours 55
Chapter 5: Wealth and Poverty in Luke's Gospel 67
Chapter 6: The Story with a Hole in It 79
Chapter 7: The Two-Story House 89
Chapter 8: The Divided City 101
Chapter 9: Where Money Doesn't Talk: The Economic
                    and Relational Gap 109
Chapter 10: Redeeming the Gaps 123
Chapter 11: The Alternative Disciples 137
Chapter 12: Reimagining the City 155
Chapter 13: Finding a New Location 169
Conclusion 177

References / 181
About the Author / 187
About Urban Loft Publishers / 188

Series Preface

Urban Mission in the 21st Century is a series of monographs that addresses key issues facing those involved in urban ministry whether it be in the slums, squatter communities, *favelas*, or in immigrant neighborhoods. It is our goal to bring fresh ideas, a theological basis, and best practices in urban mission as we reflect on our changing urban world. The contributors to this series bring a wide-range of ideas, experiences, education, international perspectives, and insight into the study of the growing field of urban ministry. These contributions fall into four very general areas: 1—the biblical and theological basis for urban ministry; 2—best practices currently in use and anticipated in the future by urban scholar/activists who are living, working and studying in the context of cities; 3—personal experiences and observations based on urban ministry as it is currently being practiced; and 4—a forward view toward where we are headed in the decades ahead in the expanding and developing field of urban mission. This series is intended for educators, graduate students, theologians, pastors, and serious students of urban ministry.

More than anything, these contributions are creative attempts to help Christians strategically and creatively think about how we can better reach our world that is now more urban than rural. We do not see theology and practice as separate and distinct. Rather, we see sound practice growing out of a healthy vibrant theology that seeks to understand God's world as it truly is as we move further into the twenty-first century. Contributors interact with the best scholarly literature available at the time of writing while making application to specific contexts in which they live and work.

Each book in the series is intended to be a thought-provoking work that represents the author's experience and perspective on urban ministry in a particular context. The editors have chosen those who bring this rich diversity of perspectives to this series. It is our hope and prayer that each book in this series will challenge, enrich, provoke, and cause the reader to dig deeper into subjects that bring the reader to a deeper understanding of our urban world and the ministry the church is called to perform in that new world.

Dr. Kendi Howells Douglas and Stephen Burris,
Urban Mission in the 21st Century Series **Co-Editors**

Other books in the Urban Ministry for the 21st Century series include:

Crossroads of the Nations: Diaspora, Globalization, and Evangelism by
Jared Looney

Dedication

For my parents, Ray and Sheila and in memory of Ted Roberts, friend and mentor.

Preface

Many of the themes in this book go back to 1999 when my family and I arrived in Nairobi for a six-year stint that ended up lasting fourteen years. Nairobi is an utterly remarkable city, offering endless encounters that have, by turn, left me disturbed, challenged, enriched, and profoundly grateful.

The danger for the foreigner in any city is that we ask more questions of places than we allow them to ask of us. I hope that in what follows I have kept some balance in my dialogue with a place I have grown to know and love. My guides in that process have been the congregation of St Jerome Church, Kibera, the staff and students of Carlile College's Centre for Urban Mission, and the community that surrounds these two places. I owe these friends a deeper debt than I can convey.

My particular thanks to Richard Mayabi, Barrack Oluoch, Imbumi Makuku, and Simon Peter Waite, who graciously shared with me insights into some of their costly experience and commitment to mission in this part of the city. Thank you, too, to Nancy Njagi Mbiithi and all those at the Centre for Urban Mission who continue to strive with the communities they serve, for the transformation they all seek.

My other guides along the way are those who have read all or part of this manuscript and provided critical feedback. I am deeply indebted to David Smith, who also provided the encouragement to write, and to Cathy Ross, Linda Martindale, Craig Stuart, and John Padwick. My thanks goes as well to the series editors, Kendi Howells Douglas and Stephen Burris, for their patience over a long journey.

The book was largely written in Cape Town, South Africa, through the generous provision of a sabbatical provided by the Church Mission Society. During my family's stay in Cape Town, we based ourselves around the Warehouse, a ministry of St. John's Parish, Wynberg, and St. Peter's Church, Mowbray. Both were places of extraordinary generosity and hospitality and a constant source of inspiration. My particular thanks goes to Craig and Liesl Stuart, Caroline Powell, and Dave and Bev Meldrum.

Throughout the process of writing there is one person who has provided an endless supply of encouragement, campaigned for commas in the right places, and pressed for greater clarity and simplicity. My wife Anita, the unofficial editor, constant supporter, and supplier of countless mugs of coffee—thank you!

Introduction
There's a Beggar at the Gate

There are moments for all of us that in some way define us. They point out, however painfully, truths about ourselves that we cannot deny and are perhaps unwilling or feel unable to change. Sometimes the heralds of those truths come from unlikely quarters, which serve to deepen our sense of unease about who we are or what we have become.

One such moment was a Saturday morning at our home in Nairobi not long after my family had arrived from Britain to work with the Anglican Church of Kenya. I was busy washing the family car when a voice called to me from our gate. Putting down the sponge, I walked across to where a disheveled man stood holding a piece of paper in his outstretched hand; another beggar at the gate. I reached for the paper but was taken aback as hands were thrust through the gate and mine were clasped by his. "Let us pray," he declared in a loud voice. My brother in Christ then lifted his eyes to heaven and his voice to any who might be in earshot and thanked the good Lord I had been so blessed with a nice house, a warm and dry place for my children, food on my table, and even a car. He then reminded God he had nothing, he had been locked out of an iron sheet hut for not paying his rent (this was explained in the contents of the piece of paper), and his children starved while mine ate. He then pleaded with the God of heaven to touch the heart of this his brother that he might be generous in this hour of need.

I have never felt so blatantly manipulated by a prayer. In my anger I insisted the prayer was not genuine, that he was using prayer as a tool to manipulate me, and this was not honoring to God. I have, thankfully, forgotten much of what I said to him but suspect that I vigorously defended a God who undoubtedly did not need defending. In truth I was defending myself because of course the prayer had been heard by the very ears it was intended for—mine. I was troubled because I was being so transparently used; I was troubled because I was a Western missionary in Africa, and it felt as if whatever I owned or enjoyed was to be contaminated by guilt. Above all, I felt troubled because whether or not the prayer was entirely honest, I had little doubt it revealed a truth about the realities of our very different lives.

In a rage, I walked into the house, grabbed my wallet, pulled out some notes, and marched back to the gate. I thrust my hands through the same gap he had used, gave him a piece of my mind along with my cash, and said I did not want him back again begging at the gate. We separated, not exactly as the best of friends, and I returned to the task of car washing with conspicuously more energy than before.

I am not someone God speaks to directly, or if I am then I generally fail to hear. But that morning was different as I sensed quite clearly God saying to me either to give graciously and willingly or to not give at all, but that I should not hurt myself and others by such ungracious words and actions. As the sponge made its way a little more slowly over the back bumper, I repented and resolved before God not to act in that manner again. Hardly had the prayer finished than there was another voice at the gate.

I tell the story not to reveal a sense of guilt at the privileges I enjoy or to disclose my capacity for living ungraciously, but to point out that being on the receiving end of begging, as most of us know, is not the easiest experience. My response did nothing for this man at the gate. A marriage of guilt and deception was never going to give birth to honesty, generosity, or justice. We both parted a little poorer, a little less than what we might have been; our humanity somehow reduced within the narrow gap at the gate that separated us.

What kind of response was needed that would not descend into such a dehumanizing encounter? A kinder and more honest conversation would have been a good place to start! But I and my brother at the gate are also part of a wider picture of a world of profound economic disparity. The gulf between us had a global dimension. How then might we create a different story, a story involving entering into these gaps and finding the spaces from which to see ourselves and each other in a truer light? And how, in that light, can we respond in ways that promote freedom and dignity and reflect God's justice? There are no easy answers to these questions, but neither can we ignore them.

In the first half of this book, we consider a parable Jesus tells about a non-encounter between a rich man and the beggar named Lazarus who lies at his gate. As we approach Luke's telling of the parable, we need to avoid sanitizing the story with sentimental notions of what it means to have a beggar on the doorstep or make judgments from the comfort of our distance from the narrative. The idea of a beggar taking up semipermanent residence outside our home is not an experience most of us would relish.

I am pointing this out as a way of introducing the awkwardness of the parable we will explore later. We might wish to have a certain sympathy, or at least an understanding, for this rich man who has a beggar parked at the end of his drive. If there is any empathy on my part towards the rich man, it is because my world seems uncomfortably close to his. Granted I do not live on gourmet food or dress in designer suits, but in the league tables of the global economy, some of us are in the house and some are at the gate, and I am uncomfortably aware of where I am located.

We live in a world that finds itself reflected in the words of the parable, where ugly distortions turn out to be accurate descriptions of the places and spaces most of us from the global north appear to occupy. We live in a world where the combined earnings of players in two international football teams exceed the Gross Domestic Product of some African nations. We live in a world where, at the end of the last millennium the assets of the world's three wealthiest people were more than the combined GDP of the 48 least-developed countries, comprising 600 million people (Castells, 2000, p. 78). It is a world where the economy of global corporations is greater than many countries.

Statistically, we live in a world where the richest 10% of adults account for 85% of the world total of global assets, while the poorest half of the world's adult population own barely 1% (Randerson, 2006). Practically, we live in a world where the cost of a Friday night take-out pizza for one family is the monthly income of another. But these statistics tell only part of the story. For in them the rich and the poor inhabit separate places and seldom meet. There may be little intersection of their lives beyond the media image, the virtual Lazarus whose sustained presence depends largely on the television remote.

Nowhere, however, is this story brought so vividly to life than in the cities of the majority world. Here, amid the rapidly emerging urban centers, global inequality and wholesale economic disparity are played out like a perverse model of a global village, where the rich man and Lazarus finally get to meet. No media is needed to tell this story, only eyes open to the realities of city life.

For 10 years my work and ministry largely centered on Kibera, one of the largest slums or informal settlements in Africa. This experience and the broader experience of life in Nairobi informs much of what follows in this book. The initial idea of connecting the parable of the beggar at the gate to life in the city is not my own but drawn from an article by Father Alex Zanotelli, a Catholic priest who spent 10 years living among the people of Korogocho, another of Nairobi's slums. In an article reflecting on life in Korogocho, Father Zanotelli describes Nairobi as a city where the economic inequalities create an impression of heaven and hell side by side (2002, pp. 13–17). The article contains a powerful critique of the inequalities of life in Nairobi. Yet while many have raged against the system or carefully lined up statistics and arguments, the impact of his writing comes through not being an observer or commentator, but from the realities of his life lived among the poor.

Very early in my time in Nairobi I spent an afternoon with Father Alex walking round the community and chatting in the small mud and iron sheet hut that he occupied. I wondered how, in such a place, he survived emotionally and spiritually, sensing I myself lacked the inner resources for the path he had taken. In the end, I found the courage to ask him. He looked at me, with more than half a smile, and cryptically replied, "If God exists, he can only be found in Korogocho." He said no more and left me to work it out from there. He was neither doubting God's existence nor making extravagant claims for spiritual enlightenment in what was then the most difficult and dangerous slum in Kenya. Rather, I suspect he was offering an insight into the spirituality that had nurtured his own difficult and challenging vocation. In whatever place we find ourselves, in whatever circumstances, we can discover the riches of God's grace and the resources to sustain our calling.

My encounter with Father Alex was important because, confronted with one small corner of the world's profound injustices, he seemed to have found a way to live out his faith and calling with integrity and purpose. His brief written reflection points above all to the way his own life, vocation, and experience of God were profoundly challenged and in some ways reordered and renewed through encounters and relationships with those who occupied the underside of history. As I returned that evening to my wife and two children, I knew my life would not follow the same path as his. There are those around the world who have responded to a call to relocate and make their home, perhaps for a season of their lives, in the most difficult and often dangerous places in order to share the life of the poor and seek the transformation of the communities that become their home. Those of us who have not walked that path, or who have in the past but find ourselves in a different place now, remain confronted with the questions of what it means to live with integrity and purpose in a world marred by poverty and injustice.

Charles Elliott (1985) describes the dual jaws of a trap from which many of us struggle to extricate ourselves. One jaw is the debilitating pressure of guilt, which my visitor at the gate seemed able to touch so effectively. The other is a sense of powerlessness, which leaves us in danger of either ignoring or justifying the realities around us, because we cannot change them. Conversely, we may resort to a kind of activism whose driving force seems rooted in unacknowledged feelings of guilt or a basic desire to do something, which masks our deeper sense of powerlessness. I cannot claim to have escaped either of these jaws. However, my aim in this book is, from the Gospel of Luke, to reflect on what it might mean as a Christian to live faithfully and with integrity and purpose in the face of the ever-widening inequalities of the global economy.

If my years in Kenya have taught me anything, these fundamental questions of Christian lifestyle cannot be tackled alone. Western individualism so often leads us to ask critical questions about our identity, role, and purpose in the world. Unhelpfully, however, this often leaves us with a sense of something to be addressed at the level of our own person or household, somehow independently from the community to which we belong. Kenya has reminded me I cannot discover the answers to such questions alone, but only in the company of others.

Much has been made of the contrast between Descartes's dictum, *I think, therefore I am*, and an African worldview encapsulated in the words, *I am, because we are*. This African philosophy, closely associated with the concept of ubuntu, stresses that our identity is rooted in and bound up in relationships with others. It resonates with a biblical perspective far more than the European Enlightenment thinking that colors the way many of us see and interpret the world. Like a computer operating system, it runs unnoticed in the background, yet all we encounter is processed through it.

The writers of the Gospels inhabited a very different world, a world where such individualistic thinking would be largely alien. Within their context, and in greater proximity to an African worldview, the self was also understood in relationship to others.

For all the value of individual reflection and contemplation, the fundamental questions of how we are to live faithfully and with integrity in a divided world cannot be examined in isolation. We must find answers from conversations within a community of faith, and perhaps more than ever, within a global community of faith that questions us, our values, perceptions, and beliefs in ways that must ultimately challenge us to move closer to the way and person of Christ.

In the following chapters we will look at the way cities can be contexts marked by social and economic divides and the way Luke's Gospel both reflects and challenges those divisions. We will consider the realities and structures of the divided city, which are starkly manifest in the parable of the rich man and Lazarus, but equally evident within the Gospel as a whole. Against the background of an oppressive and fragmented society, Luke portrays Jesus as one who transcends and transforms the gaps that lie at the heart of human experience. Reflecting on this Jesus who we encounter in Luke, I hope we will discover ways to navigate the "gaps" and divides of our times and live more faithfully in God's world.

Most of us are familiar with the nagging doubts that can gnaw at the very roots of our sense of purpose and intention. I have found this particularly true when faced with writing this book. Let me confess my own doubts at this early stage. The question that has accompanied me throughout the journey of writing, at times challenging me to give up and walk away from the project, has been the gap between the things I aspire to and the reality of my life and my family's experience.

I would love to write in a way that demonstrates I have embodied and lived out the conclusions that I reach, but I know I am very far from that. The right to write, if such a thing is required, comes only from the reality of entering into these gaps and struggling to make sense of them. Navigating the gaps requires courage; joyful, redemptive imagination; and a sacrificial commitment that longs to remain true to our calling in spite of the cost. I constantly encounter those who tread that path far more faithfully than I do. I will tell some of their stories along the way. But in my constant return to Luke's Gospel, I find myself faced with the simplest and most difficult of conclusions. This redemptive transforming work, the healing of a fragmented world and divided cities, lies in a constant recovery, in the realities of our own lives and communities, of what it means to respond to Jesus's gracious and costly invitation: "Follow me."

Chapter 1

Approaching the City

Only people who are constantly being changed can bring change to others.

--Simon Barrington-War

Arrival

"Welcome to Nairobi!" A stranger who will become a friend greets us at the airport. Our names in bold letters on a piece card provide the comforting knowledge that we are at least expected if not actually known. Luggage is transported to the awaiting car, and we begin the journey, one I will subsequently make on numerous occasions, from the airport to the city center. I still have parts of our initial journey etched in my mind, memories of glancing through the windows with the unsettling experience of trying to adjust to the idea that this was about to become our new home. Places I now know well can, at least in my imagination, be seen again as if for the first time with its strangeness and newness.

The early months of endeavoring to feel at home in a radically new environment are often awkward and confusing. Reading through my journal of those initial weeks and months, my sense of dislocation, confusion, and self-doubt are all too evident. Yet I suspect the early months critically affect the way we engage with a new place and people and lay foundations for a life in a new environment that can be difficult to reconfigure later. So often it can be events, positive or negative, and our initial responses to them and the people associated with them, that shape how we learn to live in a new place. The challenge of the unfamiliar leads us to a number of reactions that shape our future engagement with the city.

Cities are almost by definition cross-cultural environments, creating the potential for innumerable experiences of encountering others whose cultures, personal histories, beliefs, values, and lifestyles may be radically different from our own. Richard Sennet (1990) notes:

> The modern city can turn people outward, not inward; rather than wholeness, the city can give them experiences of otherness. The power of the city to reorient people in this way lies in its diversity; in the presence of difference people have at least the opportunity to step outside themselves. (p. 123)

Yet very often we fail to seize that opportunity. Instead we engage with cities in ways that insulate us from the diversity of experiences and people found there. We may seek to find refuge in the known and familiar and find ways to distance our lives from the people and places that are more alien to us. In doing so, of course, we are retreating from the very nature of urban life.

Embracing the Difference

The first cities were born in the ancient world of Mesopotamia, sometime in the 3rd century BCE. They were born from an epoch of revolution that changed the way people came together and organized themselves (Hollis, 2013, p. 17). In the city, we see the emergence of writing and accounting, the creation of diverse skills, technologies and arts, and the diversity of people and of economic and social activity. The philosopher Kwame Appiah celebrates this urban diversity in what he terms cosmopolitanism. For him, this diversity contains within it a moral imperative, for in this cosmopolitan world we have obligations to others that go beyond relationships of blood and nationality, requiring us to take seriously the value of the lives of others (Fainstein, 2010, p. 174).

This process of coming into closer proximity with people who are different from us provides not only opportunity but some responsibility. We become our brother's keeper among people who in many respects may be nothing like the brother or sister we know. In the urban community, the question "Who is my neighbor?" demands a new answer (Davey, 2002, p. 8). The challenge of the city is to love the neighbor, when this neighbor is fundamentally a stranger to us.

In the sometimes transitory or contractual nature of some relationships in urban life, there is, critically, obligation that is not limited to those with whom our relationships are deeper and more intimate. There are echoes here of the African concept of *ubuntu*, of acknowledging our life and identity are somehow bound up in the life of others. We may also find here echoes of Luke 10 and Jesus's discussion of who constitutes our neighbor. What are the demands of neighborliness in a complex world where categories of stranger and neighbor collide in the person we encounter on the road? There is much in our experience of urban life that resists this mutuality, this obligation and openness to unknown others. This can lead us to positions of defensiveness and levels of seclusion. One primary cause of this is fear.

Shut the Gate

Day one of our arrival in Nairobi, and we are moved into our new home. It is a bungalow, or at least half of one, the guest wing of the original building that has now been divided into two homes. We drop our bags near the door, check out the mattresses on the floor, which will suffice till we find beds, and begin to wonder what life will be like in this place. Outside I leave the gate wide open onto the road. I sense somehow this new home with its boundary fence is offering an island of space and security for our family yet cutting us off from life outside the gate.

Moments later, Moses appears. He works for our neighbor, and he seems somewhat agitated. "You must shut the gate!" I am taken aback by his sense of urgency. There appears to be no threat on the street outside. We have never lived behind locked gates, and I don't intend to start now. I raise my objections, but the conversation is short-lived as Moses makes clear that he will shut the gate if I don't. My open gate threatens both our security and our neighbor's, Moses's employer. The gate is locked, our world is secure, but I feel diminished in the process. This small battle lost is part of a wider process that will define my relationship to this as yet unknown city of Nairobi.

The padlocked gate serves as a metaphor of how we can relate to the world around us. Cities offer, at least for some of us, the possibility of living life in isolation from the wider environment in which we find ourselves. To withdraw, to shut the gate, to identify the safe places, emotionally, physically, and even spiritually from which we can encounter the city leads to the fragmentation of urban life and ultimately impoverishes ourselves and those around us. Secure in our particular in-car-nations we can encounter urban life through the climate-controlled environment of the private vehicle, hermetically sealed from the world lying beyond the windscreen, passing through places which we will never actually encounter and by people we will never meet (C. Smith, 2011).

Our commitment to mission requires a very different relationship to the city, which must somehow refuse the fragmentation and the insulation from the unknown other. It is a refusal that must above all be embodied within the life of the church.

Belonging

Peter Selby (1991), a former bishop of Kingston, in South London, once described the church as the "first fruit of God's longing" (p. 3). As such, he saw the church as a visible expression of God's longing for the whole created order to be transformed. Divine longing, Selby argued, produces new forms of belonging in a church that is called to transcend and heal the boundaries of a broken society. God's longing creates new possibilities for our belonging.

Yet our experience of church is so often far from ideal. Instead we live within the tension of our own longings for what might be and the joys and frustrations of belonging to what is. The reality of being an expression of God's longing and the vocation to bear witness to his work in redeeming creation makes the church different from other forms of human community. Yet in other respects we are a community like so many others, caught between higher ideals and our basic desire to find a sense of place and belonging.

The city in some respects represents this tension on a larger scale. The diverse longings and interests that shape our creation of urban space do not always sit easily with the impulse to find contexts for community, relationship, and belonging which embrace the many and not the privileged few. Open spaces that do not generate economic return are constantly under pressure. The park I once looked out onto, when living in inner London, is now reduced and obscured by a block of apartments. The city has been described by Susan Fainstein as humanity's most successful attempt to model the world "after his heart's desire" (2010, p. 171). Yet, caught within the contemporary realities of global capitalism, cities are ever prone to develop in ways that create structures of exclusion rather than belonging.

Cities can represent the possibility of living in closer community amid greater diversity. At the time of writing, I am living in the Observatory area of Cape Town. Its history is as one of South Africa's few "gray areas" in the era of apartheid. It offered the possibility for different races to live in close proximity at a time when, elsewhere in the city and the nation, the Group Areas Act enforced racial segregation. The agent who showed us into the apartment described the area as being short of light. Her reference was simply to the fact that the houses in this area were more closely packed than the suburbs to the south (although vastly more spacious in terms of where the majority of Cape Town's population live). Observatory illustrates the way urban life can be beneficially marked by both proximity and diversity.

However, the question remains as to whether urban life, marked by community and diversity, reflects our heart's desire. On the one hand, we yearn for intimacy and community and find stimulation in the different and the unexpected. Jane Jacobs notes the way urban life reflects the way we desire diversity and that diversity makes cities live. Yet on the other hand, Gans reminds us that we also cherish suburban ideals of space, privacy, and the comfort of living in more homogenous neighborhoods, where people share a similar socioeconomic status or background (Gans, as cited by Fainstein, 2010).

Cities therefore offer the opportunity for diverse groups of people to live in closer proximity. Yet they also represent the atomization of life as we build worlds for ourselves in isolation from others or from those who are particularly "other" to us. New arrivals to a city like Nairobi, particularly expatriates, can quickly find ways of living life in a manner that never intersects with the majority of the population. We soon develop our own geographies, our internal maps of the city that connect us to places where we feel at home, while providing a deeper dislocation from the places we don't. We shut the gate on the places remote from our own experience. It sometimes appears that the locks on the gate become rusted to the point that the possibility of ever opening them into another world seems too remote to consider, too unsafe to undertake. The gate becomes just an extension of the fence and the insularity is complete. When the otherness of the city impinges upon us, we then learn to greet it with cynicism and contempt, or just plain fear.

Come and See

Two months into our time in Nairobi, and I am struggling to get a grasp of Swahili. In some ways it is the language of the street. English is the language of school and office. Mother tongue languages are spoken at home, but on the street, where different ethnic groups rub shoulders with each other, Swahili is the lingua franca. My helper in this task is Moses from next door. We sit on the steps outside a shared back door, and I try to practice what has been learned in the day. Amid the conversation, we talk about his life in Nairobi. He lives in Kibera, Nairobi's most infamous slum or, more accurately, informal settlement. He talks about the place for awhile and then asks if I would like to visit. Sure I reply, why not? It was a simple invitation, but it radically changed not only those first months but the 14 years that followed.

Prior to Kenya, I had lived and worked in London's inner city, initially in Bermondsey just south of Tower Bridge, and later a few miles further out near Forest Hill. Nothing I had witnessed there prepared me for that afternoon in Kibera. Having now spent 10 years attached to a church in Kibera and a similar length of time heading up a ministry based there, it is hard to recall those first impressions without them being colored by subsequent experience. Today Kibera is a place associated with friends and communities that have enriched and renewed my life. But on my first day, the experience was one of shock and horror. Contexts define us in some way, and seeing Moses in his context left me deeply confused as I tried to reconcile the person I was coming to know with an environment that seemed so utterly alien.

For any first-time visitor, Kibera is a visceral experience, an onslaught on the senses. It is a seeming ocean of iron sheet roofs, dissected by narrow alleys and open sewers, and home to myriads of families in single-room, 10-by-10-foot houses. Perhaps my greatest shock at the time was that Moses paid rent on his room. I later discovered being a slum landlord is one of the most lucrative investments in Nairobi with absentee, largely politically connected landlords making substantial profits from minimal investments. Ninety-five percent of the structure owners of Nairobi's slums are absentee landlords living outside the slums (Dafe, 2009). At the time, I simply could not comprehend either how my unofficial Swahili teacher could survive in such an environment or how he could unquestioningly pay rent on a room that seemed to lack any service or provision for which one could justifiably charge a fee. More critically, I could not see why he would choose to stay there when he had a room on his employer's compound. I needed to learn more about Kibera than a one-hour visit could possibly reveal.

The outcome of that visit was a three year journey that led me to become an assistant pastor of a church in Kibera and to work with a theological college in developing a training center in the heart of the community. There are moments when God extends his grace to us in encounters we have never planned and could never have conceived. I look back on that day as a gift, as a moment of the Holy Spirit's prompting. But I also find myself returning to the questions that initial experience asked of me then that, even now, remain unanswered.

Minding the Gap

Those unanswered questions center on the struggle to grasp what it means for us as Christians and as churches, as the fruit of God's longing, to live authentically and with integrity in a world of profound economic division. What does that reality ask of us? How are we to respond to it?

Much of my reflection on these questions comes from my experience of Nairobi. However, the reality of cities as places of economic disparity is global and certainly not confined to any continent or region. Urban injustice is fundamentally a global phenomenon. Edward Soja (2010) notes, "As the whole world becomes urbanised and globalised to some degree, the urbanization of injustice and the globalisation of injustice reinforce one another to create what are probably the greatest inequalities of wealth and power the world has ever seen" (p. 60). Questions about justice cannot be considered independently of urbanization, not only because the majority of the world's population now lives in cities, but above all, according to Erik Swyngedouw, because the city condenses the manifold tensions and contradictions infusing modern life (Swyngedouw, as cited by Soja,

2010, p. 1). Cities are places where critical questions of justice and the equitable distribution of resources are played out every day.

In the following pages, I will use Luke's Gospel as a lens through which to look at the city and at issues of economic justice. It might be argued that a two-thousand-year-old book hardly represents the clearest or most contemporary lens to look at something as complex as the modern city. So why Luke's Gospel?

Some years ago, a visitor to the Centre for Urban Mission in Kibera looked at the different types of ministry we were engaged in and then asked which book or writer had been most influential in shaping and giving some kind of framework to our thinking. Without a moment's hesitation, I replied, Luke. If I look back at the sermons and Bible studies I have prepared over the past few years, I have to confess an over dependency on Luke's Gospel, with Isaiah coming in a close second. I hope the reason why I particularly focus on Luke and the book's relevance to questions of urban justice and injustice will become apparent. In particular, the parable of the rich man and Lazarus provides rich pickings for that discussion, but it needs to be seen within a wider discussion of the Gospel and the social context that Luke describes. We now turn to that social and economic context.

Mind the Gap

Chapter 2
Behind the Scenes: Luke's Context and Ours

Because I know that time is always time
And place is always and only place
And what is actual is actual only for one time
And only for one place.

--T.S. Eliot, "Ash Wednesday"

A Different Kind of Gap

Before we delve into Luke's Gospel, we need to address two gaps that confront us as we seek to let Luke speak into our context. The first is to acknowledge the gap that exists between the world that Luke describes and the world we inhabit. It can be all too easy to read into Luke's Gospel our own experience as if Luke is himself a product of the 21st century. At some level we cannot avoid doing that. As we read Luke, we interpret him through the lens of our own experience. Even familiar words like "rich" and "poor" or "village" and "city" will be understood and imagined from the perspectives of our own times and places. If we are to better grasp Luke's Gospel, we need to be aware of those gaps between our worlds and try not to read our world into Luke's, but instead try to read his world into ours. Sean Freyne (2004) captures the problem very well. "Imaginings of the past always involve our awareness of the present, and to the extent that the figure of Jesus can be made to support our own best insights and dreams it is difficult to avoid the temptation of co-opting him for our cause" (p. 5). To avoid this we need to get a richer understanding of the context in which Luke's Gospel is set.

But there is another gap we need to navigate. This is not the gap between our time and place and that of Luke's Gospel, but rather the gap between Luke's own context and the one he describes. Luke is the most self-consciously historical of all the evangelists (Freyne, 2004, p. 18). Yet he is possibly writing 50 years after Jesus for an audience that may have been very different to the one we encounter in his Gospel.

Karl Allen Kuhn (2010) argues persuasively that Luke is writing from a position of privilege, as a social elite, to those who similarly hold an elite status. He goes on to suggest that the thrust of Luke's Gospel is to challenge his fellow elite to abandon all for the sake of Christ (p. 105). In a Gospel that so clearly articulates the voice of the poor and so uncomfortably warns of the dangers of wealth, this may appear an odd perception of Luke and his audience. Yet it is likely that Luke is challenging an elite readership to consider what it really means to join the Christian movement and be drawn into a relationship with Christ and with others, a relationship not defined by privileged social location and patronage or one's proximity to Caesar and the Palestinian aristocracy (p. 105). His Gospel becomes deeply prophetic and in that respect all the more relevant to those of us who read it from a similar position of privilege.

Observing the gap in time and social location, and perhaps the particular angle Luke has on the Jesus story, need not lead us to doubt the historicity of Luke's account. Certainly there are those from a distance of two millennia who have sought to reconstruct Gospel narratives as if such a vast gap of time and place affords them a more privileged position to recreate the life of Christ than that available to the four evangelists. Instead, while recognizing that Luke is writing for a different audience to the one he describes, we need to do justice to the historicizing tendency of the evangelists and most particularly to Luke's stated intention of delivering an "orderly account" (Freyne, 2004, p. 5).

Seeing Jesus Through Another's Eyes

One of my favorite training resources consists of a pack of postcards made up of pictures of Jesus created by artists from all around the world. It is a remarkable collection of portraits that facilitates the exploration of who Jesus is to us and the images we have of him. In the pictures, we see Jesus as Korean, American, Brazilian, Kenyan, Filipino —a Jesus of many different races and cultures. In contemplating the images, it is those of a Jesus who is so different and other from me that remind me that my internal, often unacknowledged, images are also refracted through the light of my culture and place in history.

One exercise involving the cards is to spread them out on the floor and give people time to select the picture that most speaks to them of who Jesus is. In the conversations following the exercise, it is common to hear people discussing the way they have found some pictures to be deeply troublesome, even offensive. Frequently it is the pictures of Jesus tortured and in pain, or a Jesus who is profoundly angry that create the strongest negative reactions. These pictures are generally the work of Christian artists living in contexts of political and economic oppression and fear. They present us with stark images of a Jesus who identifies with their agony and suffering.

It is hard for some of us to recognize that these uncomfortable portrayals of Jesus may reflect a much truer picture of him than the more serene images we may carry within us. Certainly they will have been painted from a context much closer to Jesus's experience than that of most Europeans or North Americans.

We may conjure up in our mind's eye images of Jesus in contexts of rural tranquillity, "O Sabbath rest by Galilee! O calm of hills above," yet in reality Jesus ministered in a context of massive social dislocation, increasing economic distress, and amid a rising tide of anger and resistance (D. Smith, 2011, p. 173).

In Luke, we find Jesus entering into a world in the grip of a social and economic crisis (Moxnes, 1988, p. 73). Even in the record of his birth, Luke reminds us that this is an age of empire, where Israel is dominated by Roman rule. While Matthew will point us to the prophetic fulfillment of Jesus's place of birth, Luke will also show us that Joseph and Mary find themselves on the road to Bethlehem through the imperial decree of Caesar Augustus (Luke 2:1).

Living in the Shadow of the Empire

Israel lived in the shadow of an empire whose tendrils reached into every aspect of life, including, as we have seen, the birth of the Messiah (Horsley, 2008). Yet what we see so powerfully in Luke is the way Jesus enters history as the one who, in his very being, transcends all the vain pretentions of the empire. Caesar Augustus was regarded as more than the head of a vast empire. He held titles like Divine, Son of God, Lord, Redeemer, and Savior. Yet in the opening chapters of Luke's Gospel, these illusions of divine power and the imperial demands of absolute allegiance are cast aside in the revelation of the one who is truly the Son of God (Luke 1:35) and a Savior and Lord (Luke 2:11).

To shepherds on a hillside there comes a message of good news. For first-century Jews at the time of Jesus, the idea of good news had two meanings. With roots in Isaiah, it pointed to God's victory over evil and the rescue of his people. However, in the Roman world it referred to the accession or birthday of the emperor (N.T. Wright, 2004, p. 307). In Luke, these two ideas are brought together as God's victory and rescue is revealed in the birth of one whose kingship far surpasses that of the emperor.

From the lips of Simeon and Anna we learn that the child who is born is the glory of Israel and the hope for captive Israel's redemption. We are rightly struck by the theological significance of these words, rooted as they are in God's salvation history, but this should not disguise their subversive political force in a nation longing for liberation.

Jesus was born into a society whose political and economic life was controlled by forces from beyond its boundaries yet active at the very heart of the political, economic, and even religious institutions of its day. For a covenant people who were bound to the one true God, this was most tragically seen at the highest levels of religious life. Within the temple itself, the High Priest was appointed by the Roman governor and temple staff held the responsibility of collecting tributes for Rome (D. Smith, 2011, p. 188). Richard Horsley (2008) notes that more than the Herodian kings and the Roman governors, it was the temple-state, with its high-priestly aristocracy in their lavish mansions, who eventually constituted "the face of Roman imperial rule in Judea" (p. 80). Similarly, Freyne observes, "The Galilean Jewish peasant found himself in the rather strange position that those very people to whom he felt bound by ties of national and religious loyalty, the priestly aristocracy, were in fact his social oppressors" (Freyne, as cited by C. Meyers, 2008, p. 52). We should hardly be surprised, therefore, that while the crowd joyfully celebrated Jesus's entry into Jerusalem, Jesus's own response is one of grief, weeping over a city that had abandoned her divine calling.

This distortion of the role of the temple also creates a certain irony around Jesus's statement to give to Caesar what belongs to Caesar and to God what belongs to God (Luke 20:25). While the questioning leading up to the statement was aimed to trap Jesus, in reality, Jerusalem's religious elite had rendered all to Caesar. A temple intended as a central storehouse in an economy geared towards the redistribution of God's abundant provision had come instead to represent something altogether different (C. Meyers, 2008, p. 79). Rather than meeting the needs of the aliens, orphans, and widows, as well as supporting the priesthood, it provided tribute to Rome and funded a priestly aristocracy. It is against this background that we need to understand Jesus's cleansing of the temple, where we see him in confrontation with the confluence of the economic, religious, and political forces of his day.

Naming the Powers

Early in Luke's Gospel, we catch a glimpse of this unholy alliance of powers, of kings, governors, and priests who owe their positions and allegiance to Rome. When Luke wants to provide us with a chronological reference for who is in power at the onset of John the Baptist's ministry (Luke 3:1-2), he provides the names of the emperor and his prefect, the Herodian kings, and the high priesthood in Jerusalem. Surely this is too much detail, even for someone seeking to provide an orderly account? But these are not simply chronological references. They represent the structures of political and economic power of his day.

Beneath the Roman imperial structure in Palestine there were effectively two further tiers of government, the Herodian kings and the priestly elite in Jerusalem (D. Smith, 2011, p. 174). When Jesus announced in the synagogue in Nazareth that he had come to preach good news to the poor, he was declaring it to an audience obliged to pay taxes to all three of those sources—to Rome itself, to the Herodian kings, and to the priesthood in the form of tithes and offerings (D. Smith, 2011, p. 174). This placed a largely peasant population under massive economic pressure. Horsley (2008) notes, "The demand for tribute to Rome and taxes to Herod in addition to tithes and offerings to the Temple and priesthood dramatically escalated the economic pressure on peasant producers whose livelihood was perennially marginal at best" (p. 80). According to Stegman and Stegman, the consequence of this economic pressure resulted in a crisis of debt that in turn led to the loss of inherited family land and the ever-growing concentration of land in the hands of a small but wealthy elite. Land-grabbing rulers and heavy taxation were creating a chasm between rich and poor that was driving small farmers, day laborers, fishermen, shepherds, widows, and orphans into absolute poverty and despair (as cited by D. Smith, 2011, p. 174).

What we see, therefore, is an ever-widening gap between rich and poor, in a society where the centers of wealth and power dominate a periphery struggling with poverty, landlessness, and debt. Within that structure, the central institution of Israel's life, the temple and its clerical aristocracy, appears to have been captivated by the spirit of the empire and coopted in its service.

This struggle to survive at the periphery of life against oppressive forces, seen and unseen, is graphically illustrated today in the nightmare of slum evictions. Around the world whole communities, living at the margins of urban life, struggle to maintain a toehold in cities where their most basic human rights are often ignored or dispensed with in favor of other, more powerful interests. There are few more distressing sights, anywhere in the world, than families stranded on pavements and roadsides amid meager possessions while their home is repossessed or demolished.

Powerlessness in the Face of the Powers

I arrived in Mukuru slum in Nairobi just as the bulldozers were leaving. The smell of tear gas was still in the air and stung our eyes. The heavy machinery had arrived in the middle of the night, catching the community unawares. By early morning, they were ripping their way through the hastily evacuated iron-sheet homes and businesses. Three people died, one from gunshot wounds from the police, whose role seemed to be to protect the interests of those behind the demolitions in the face of the inevitable wrath of the community.

Alongside colleagues from the Kenya Jubilee campaign, I walked through the devastated area, passing the skeletal remains of what was once a settled and industrious community. We watched the mass exodus of families, carrying their few belongings on hand carts. The bulldozer had only taken a couple hundred homes, but fear was doing the rest. People were leaving in droves, some removing the iron sheet walls and roofs in an attempt to salvage something from the devastation that once was home. Others just sat in family groups by the side of the road, deep in despair, with no place to go. While the community railed at the police and the drivers of the bulldozers, who were essentially following orders, the powers behind the demolition, those with a personal interest in land occupied by a community for decades, remained hidden, carefully protected from the public eye.

Talking with people who have experienced slum eviction is profoundly disturbing. Very often people who have been evicted migrate to other similarly vulnerable communities because the rents will be cheaper and because there will always be those who will take advantage of large groups of people, sometimes in their thousands, who need immediate accommodation.

David was one such person. Following an earlier eviction he had moved into Kibera to a privately rented shack on government land where houses were quite literally marked for eviction. He knew his present house was due for demolition as part of a government-sponsored slum upgrade program, but it was available and affordable for his family.

As we sat in a local Anglican Church that had provided shelter to those made homeless, he explained how he had left for work early in the morning. He was employed in the informal sector on a meager and unreliable income. He arrived at his place of work that morning only to be told to run home immediately because the demolitions had begun. By the time he got home, it was too late. His house was gone. Unlike Mukuru, this was a demolition that was prompted not by personal gain, but by a process intended to improve the housing conditions of the wider community. Yet even this process of development can represent deeper marginalization for others, particularly for those whose life in the city is most tenuous and whose circumstances are most vulnerable.

Living in the Fourth World

Stories like David's remind us of the fragility of lives at the periphery, which are marked by vulnerability and insecurity. His eviction, like thousands of others, resulted in the temporary separation of his family, who could not all be accommodated in the same place, and the disruption of his children's education. David, like millions of others around the world, represents what Manuel Castells (2008) describes as the Fourth World. Unlike the concept of Third World, which is defined by nations, even continents, the Fourth World exists in every nation, in cities on every continent, and are the "multiple black holes of social exclusion throughout the planet." Those in the Fourth World are not the victims of Roman imperialism, but part of the much wider global picture that Castells terms "informational global capitalism" (p. 168).

In words of remarkable similarity, Horsley and Castells (2008) describe the lives of those at the social and economic margins, separated by 2,000 years of history yet rooted in a common dehumanizing experience. Horsley notes how under imperial Rome the economic base of the Galilean peasantry had been so exhausted that "families and village communities began to disintegrate." Herod the Great's egocentric building campaigns, funded by over-taxation, and those of his son Herod Antipas, had decimated the peasant economy in Galilee who increasingly lost control of their lands. The basic structures of their society were threatened by poverty, debt, and growing marginalization.

Castells observes a similar but contemporary crisis and one of global magnitude, evidenced by poverty and social breakdown. Describing the growing dereliction of inner-city ghettos of American cities, the crisis of family life, the impoverishment of social networks, and the disintegration of traditional societies throughout the world, he paints a picture that, tragically, is not too dissimilar to the consequences of the oppressive economic structures imposed on the poor of Jesus's day.

In earlier decades, Liberation theologians prophetically drew our attention to the similarity between this reality in the time of Jesus and their own situation in Latin America. This resemblance, notes Jon Sobrino (1978), was not simply about the context of poverty and exploitation but also about the perception and awareness of it, particularly by the institutions of religion (p. 12). Liberation theologians brought the church's attention to the way it had similarly been compromised and co-opted within the structures of oppression in their day.

From its emergence in the 1960s in Latin America, Liberation theology provided a challenge to the Roman Catholic Church to examine whom it fundamentally identified with in contexts of revolution, poverty, and oppression. Political climates have changed and some of the Marxist analysis within Liberation theology and its methods of biblical interpretation have come under much scrutiny. However, the fundamental question of where the church locates itself in contexts devoid of equity and justice remains as valid as ever. That question of location becomes imperative. It is not simply about taking sides in matters of injustice, but also about locating ourselves in ways that enable us to perceive the world and hear the Scriptures read by those who see and experience life from the periphery.

In a globalizing world of ever-powerful centers and vast economic peripheries, the question of location becomes ever more critical for those of us comfortably distant from Castell's Fourth World. We have to face the question of how much our sense of reality is derived from our position of privilege. Ched Meyers (2008) makes this rather uncomfortable observation: "Facing the truth is exceedingly difficult for those of us who by race, sex or class are the 'rightful inheritors' of the imperial project—or who at the very least are promised a comfortable metropolitan existence in exchange for our political conformity" (p. 6).

Chapter 3
A World of Us and Them

Us and Them
And after all we're only ordinary men
Me, and you.

--Pink Floyd, "Us and Them"

In Luke's Gospel, we see groups of people who in different ways are located at the margins of the world Luke describes. Their marginalization may be economic, due to poverty and debt, social, living as outsiders and outcasts, or even geographic, located away from centers of power and influence. Sometimes it is a combination of all three factors. They might, somewhat starkly, be observed in the binary relationships of lender and debtor, insider and outsider, upper and lower, city and village, inside and outside the walls, and patron and client.

Lender and Debtor

While living in Bermondsey, in central London, I was part of a Bible study group that met in our home. It was one of the most diverse groups I have ever had the privilege to be part of. It contained young graduates from Cambridge University who lived locally and helped in a nearby youth project, others who could trace their family's presence in the community for generations, and more recent arrivals from West Africa. One member of the group was Mary. She was among those with generations of history in the area. Her memory stretched back to the years between the wars when life had been particularly hard in a community whose livelihood was largely linked to the economy of the docks on the south side of the river. One of Mary's favorite stories centered on the pawn broker who served as the supplier of much of the short-term credit in her community. When money was short at the end of the week, her mother would give her some item of value to take to the broker who would exchange it for cash on the basis that the item would be bought back, in better times, with interest.

Pawnbrokers could have a very exploitative relationship with a community constantly short of cash. However, for some brokers, relationships and trust were also part of the currency in which they traded. Mary used to tell of how, when things were really tight, she would be sent to the pawnbrokers with nothing more than a drying up cloth wrapped around a house brick, so something that at least appeared substantial was taken into the shop! Her family would be given credit against something that had almost no value, neither sentimental nor monetary.

The 2008 economic crisis saw nations around the world tip off the edge of an economic precipice into a hole of gargantuan proportions as it was realized that an endless supply of credit had been secured against something of even less substance than Mary's house brick. Today many nations struggle with levels of sovereign debt expressed in numbers that are too big for some of us to visualize. The impact has been massive on the global economy, with spin-offs in terms of aid and investment that have had repercussions around the world.

We live in a world far from immune to the realities of debt. For many in the Western world debt represents a major source of anxiety, the threat or reality of unemployment, reduced diet, and a significant downsizing in almost all aspects of lifestyle. It is a painful reality. Yet it is still far removed from the effects of debt as experienced in much of the developing world, where grinding debt will drive children out of school, prevent access to healthcare, and result in a complete loss of livelihood, land, and property. In some parts of the world, debt forces people into economic relationships that are barely distinguishable from patterns of slavery. It is this latter experience of debt that we need to keep in mind as we return to the context of Luke's Gospel.

The reality of debt and the peasants' loss of their land are observable in Luke's Gospel in the frequent references to debts and loans, and in the parables, where illustrations are drawn from landowner and tenant relationships. In Luke 7:41 we encounter the moneylender who graciously cancels unpayable debts, while in Luke 12:58–59 a less forgiving and perhaps more typical scenario is described. Elsewhere, in Luke 16:1–9, we are presented with a dishonest but canny servant who uses unorthodox means to preserve a future for himself in the community by an evidently unauthorized project of debt reduction. Some commentators suggest the steward was either cutting out his own commission, or even removing an extortionate interest rate, forbidden under Jewish law. Whatever the means that produced these large figures, he ingratiates himself with his master's debtors by making some swift and calculated adjustments to the books.

In the sermon on the plain in Luke 6, we see the repeated reference to the reality of debt and the hope and necessity of forgiveness of debt. Jesus's would-be followers are encouraged to give without the expectation of repayment and to lend without expecting anything back (Luke 6:30, 6:35). We can safely assume this was not an easy message for the original hearers any more than it is for us today.

We also find this focus on debt and debt forgiveness in Luke's version of the Lord's Prayer. Here Jesus teaches the disciples to pray that their sins may be forgiven by their Heavenly Father in the same way they forgive the debts of those indebted to them. In other words, he uses the language and practice of forgiveness of debt as both a pointer to and response to God's forgiveness of sin. As Jesus prays for the coming of God's Kingdom, his prayer recorded in Luke 11:2–4 focuses on two of the fundamental needs of those around him, enough food to stay alive and the reality of spiraling debts (Horsley, 2009, p. 81).

Insiders and Outsiders

In our congregation in Bermondsey were a group of older ladies who had been part of the congregation for as long as anyone could remember. One of them was Kitty. On one occasion she recounted a visit she had from a researcher who was trying to glean some of the social history of the area. He told her he wanted to speak to those of her generation who were from the area. Kitty was quick to respond. "Oh no, I am not from round here." The researcher was taken aback as he had been given the names of longstanding members of the community. He wondered when she had arrived in the area. Kitty explained she had moved into Bermondsey 60 years ago when she married her husband. Prior to that, she had lived less than five miles away on the other side of the river. In her mind, she was still an outsider to this community.

In many established communities, whether rural or urban, there is generally some sense of what it means to be an insider or an outsider based on the history of your relationship with that community. Sometimes you need an awful lot of history to belong!

The Norwegian scholar Halvor Moxnes (1998) sees in Luke a society marked by insiders and outsiders (p. 53). The peasant farmer, the tenant farmer, the local landlord, the religious officials are the insiders in the world Luke describes. Yet there are also the outsiders who may be rich or poor. There are those who by virtue of their poverty and destitution form groups of people at the margins of society—those in Luke 14 who are grouped together as the poor, the crippled, the blind, and the lame. Then there are those who are outside because of their ethnicity, religion, or their work—the Roman soldier, tax collector, Samaritan, and absentee landlord.

We can see so many of Jesus's parables seem to address the insiders of his day, those who form the crowd, with many parables drawing on their social and economic interactions. But when it comes to the narrative section, we see the focus move toward people in a marginal position (Moxnes, 1988, p. 56). Jesus has a particular concern for those who stand on the periphery of village life, those who either temporarily or permanently find themselves in a liminal position, on the edge of the city or village but never quite within it.

Jesus may address his parables to the crowd and at other times to Pharisees and religious leaders. But in his daily interaction it is those on the margins with whom he seems to spend most time. Similarly, many of his parables, although addressed to the crowd, are marked by references to these insider/outsider relationships. Hence, we see parables of the Pharisee and the tax collector, the rich man and Lazarus, the banquet and those who receive and those who decline the invitation, the Samaritan and the priest and Levite. In each of these, the social divisions of the two groups are evident, and yet in each the insider is invited to reconsider the perception of the outsider. So often the one characterized as being closest to the Kingdom of God is the one who in every other sense is the outsider—the tax collector, Samaritan, widow, and beggar.

Uppers and Lowers

All societies are stratified in some way, such that there are those who are close to and have significant access to resources and power and those far from them. In many societies, those distinctions overlap with aspects of race and ethnicity or religion and culture. In cities, the gaps between elite groups of people, with highly concentrated access to resources and those at the social and economic margins, appears greater than in rural communities. Sometimes the economic gaps can be vast while the geographic ones are minimal. In Mumbai, I witnessed pavement shacks constructed near the gates of luxury offices and apartments. In Bermondsey, gentrification, initially along the strip closest to the river, meant penthouse apartments worth millions of pounds were occupied within a stone's throw of dilapidated social housing. In Nairobi and Cape Town, I have often felt as if I can move between worlds and continents while only traveling a short distance from one area of the city to another.

In discussing some of these economic distinctions, Bob Linthicum (2005) describes urban life as divided between haves and have-nots. He observes the way these same divisions can be seen running through Scripture. The development theorist Robert Chambers (1997) looks at these divisions differently, describing human relationships as being patterned by dominance and subordination, with people functioning as uppers or lowers (p. 56). Uppers are those who exercise power and do so in ways that define reality for others. They create the official view of the world. For Chambers, uppers and lowers are not so much fixed categories but are defined by situation or relationship. Hence, one can be an upper in one relationship and a lower in another. A man may be at the bottom of the pile in his place of work but in relation to his wife or children may adopt a position of dominance. Everyone is an upper somewhere Chambers argues, even if it is in relation to his dog!

Luke invites us into a world that is also marked by those who have and those who have not, by differences in power and dominance and by those who are clearly uppers and lowers in the social and economic systems of the day. Orlando Costas (1989) points to the way these divisions are particularly expressed in the relationship between Jerusalem at the center and "Galilee of the Gentiles" at the margins.

Jesus's ministry took place within a social and economic context where the poor were caught in a web of hierarchical and often exploitative relationships. Those with economic power were more concerned with accumulating wealth than producing it (Moxnes,1988, p. 32). Whether they were the Roman authorities or the religious elite; whether the emperor, the landlord, the tax collector, or the Pharisee (as lovers of money); whether the powerbrokers or middlemen, the poor were pushed deeper into economic crisis through the economic structure of the day. These economic structures were largely controlled by an urban elite whose extravagant lifestyle was funded by peasant labor.

In many of Jesus's parables, therefore, we see distinctions between those who own the land and those who work it, between the owner and the tenant, the master and the servant. We see the owner of the vineyard and the tenant farmers (Luke 20:9–19); the rich man and his manager (Luke 16:1–15); the master and the servant (Luke 17:7–10); the watchful servant and the one who is "beaten with many blows" (Luke 12:35–48); and in the parable of the talents we meet a landowner who, having planted a vineyard that won't produce grapes for some years, heads off for a long time, leaving the said vineyard in the hands of tenant farmers (Luke 20:9–19). In each case, the master or owner is evidently either absent, in a far country, on a long journey, or at the very least distant from the day-to-day running of the farm or business. We have a rural economy largely controlled by a distant urban elite.

Similarly, in the parable of the great banquet (Luke 14:15–24), which we will see later has a distinctly urban setting, it is evident the ones who have the wherewithal to purchase the five yolk of oxen or who have just made a significant land purchase will not be those who will plough and till the land. Their role may be to travel to the outlying villages to inspect their goods and property, but the actual work will be done by someone else who is socially, economically, and geographically distant from them.

The City and the Village

So far we have discussed the social background to Luke's Gospel without giving much attention to the urban context. Half of the references to the city in the New Testament are found in Luke or Acts, and half of those are in Luke. However we need to tread with care at this point as Luke uses the word city (polis) to describe places such as Bethlehem or Bethsaida, which other Gospel writers refer to as villages

(Rohrbaugh, 1991, p. 126). Luke seems to use the word city in a nontechnical sense to the point that mere hamlets such as Nazareth are termed city. Also, we cannot read back into first-century Palestine our 21st-century notions of what constitutes a city. Urban communities in the context of Luke's Gospel were smaller and considerably less complex and diverse than those of our present day.

However, while the Galilean context of Jesus's ministry appears to be focused on rural communities, it would be a mistake to presume Galilee was a region untouched by urbanization. Palestine under Roman rule was subject to a process of civilization that involved the construction of towns and cities through which the Romans extended political and economic control. Herod the Great and his successors, appointed as client rulers by Rome, undertook massive building projects funded through taxation of the masses. This included the construction of cities in Galilee including Sepphoris (an hour's walk from Nazareth) and Tiberius. These urban centers and their small urban elite would have significantly impacted Jesus's followers (D. Smith, 2011).

The differences we considered earlier between uppers and lowers, those who form the center and those at the margins, are also expressed in the dynamics of relationship between village and city. The differences between the rural and urban societies of Luke's day were not of agricultural versus industrial or commercial economies. Rather the difference can be best seen in terms of center versus periphery. It was marked by unequal power relations, with the power being vested in a small urban elite who controlled the production of rural land and the extraction of the surpluses generated (Moxnes, 1988, p. 28). Their relationship with the countryside was essentially parasitic (C. Myers, 2008, p. 53). In the city, this tiny wealthy elite would display and employ their unbelievable wealth in competitions for honor among each other. They were the only group with real disposable income and essentially controlled the political and economic life of the city, usually legitimized by the priestly and clerical aristocracy.

By contrast the nonelite population of the city, those who probably made up well over 90% of the population, were constantly replenished by the dispossessed of the countryside, as the outsiders of rural life. These are the people who in the social and economic crisis of their day found themselves waiting in the market place for an employer since their lack of skills relegated them to the role of day laborer (Matt 20 1–16).

Inside and Outside the City Wall

The prominent feature of cities throughout the ancient world was the city wall. The wall of course had the practical function of providing refuge and security to the inhabitants within. Yet by that very function it provided a further dimension of social division. In medieval Europe the walls of cities had posted upon them the banns, announcements at the city gates, which proclaimed to newcomers what proper civilized and urbane life was about. The wall in this sense provided not only a barrier of security but a social or cultural barrier that preserved right of entry to those qualified to be within the city. Today the word "banns" is preserved only by churches in the announcement of an impending marriage, but in origin they formed, in some respects, the boundary markers of urban civilization (Soja, 2010). Beyond them was the pagan world.

This ancient function of the city wall is illustrated in the parable of the banquet in Luke 14. Here we see the implied presence of the city wall in the twofold injunction to bring to the banquet the poor, the crippled, the blind, and the lame in place of those who had earlier refused the invitation. In the first instruction (Luke 14:21), the servant is to search the streets and alleys of the town. Not, you note, the market squares, but the back alleys of the poorer neighborhoods. When these have come in there is room to spare, so the servant is called to go out into the roads and country lanes. This is not to extend the invitation from city to village. There would be no time. This is the invitation going out to those located outside the walls of the city who have business in the city but are not permitted to live there. Their lives are shielded from view by the protective wall of the city. Here the beggar, the unclean, the prostitute, the tanner, those kept at the margins of urban society, would be found. Jesus says they must be compelled to come in. This is not invitation by force! Rather, it represents the fact that only such forcefulness will bring into the city those who know they are excluded from its gates (Rohrbaugh, as cited in Neyrey, 1991).

How then were relationships transacted between the elite landowners who occupied the center of the city and the peasant and tenant farmers who occupied the outlying rural areas? How were relationships transacted between those who owned and controlled land and resources and those who provided the labor to work the land?

The Patron and the Client

Richard, a good friend of mine, was for awhile a pastor in Kibera. Whenever I visited his home, I could be sure I would not be the only visitor. Like most homes in Nairobi it would always take awhile to discover who belonged permanently to the household, who were staying in the home as part of an extended network of relationships, and who like me, just happened to be there at that time. Richard's house in the city was connected by deep bonds of relationship to his rural community. Those who came to stay, often for unspecified lengths of time, could be relatives, members of the same village, or a pastor who had been appointed to that village. Their visits would always require food and accommodation. They might require help getting into a school or a college, finding a job, getting someone admitted to hospital or navigating government offices. I guess the bus fare home might also have occasionally been on the list.

On one occasion, early in my time in Kenya, I was struggling to understand how to make proper use of our own more substantial resources in the face of various requests for help with anything from funeral expenses to school fees. I asked him how it fitted into the way he organized his giving. He looked at me and laughed, "That isn't giving, that is just life!"

For the colleagues I worked with, these relationships were part of the daily reality of their lives and represented their connectedness to wider bonds of family and community. They had access to what one writer describes as the "thickening fields of social relations" that help make urban life in Africa viable (Simone, 2005, p. 1). These bonds are deeply relational, but they have a strong economic component.

Whether in Nairobi's slums or more affluent estates, the majority of the population there, by virtue of a presumed wealth associated with life in the city, would be supporting, housing, or paying school fees for any number of people. The weight of expectation contained within those relationships was often a massive strain on households that could barely support themselves. Yet for many, the fulfillment of these obligations was not only a burden but arose from an inherent sense of duty and responsibility. Many of those helped would be relatives, but not all. The relationship was essentially redistributive, a sharing of some of the surplus generated by urban living. Those arriving from the village would often come with groundnuts, maize, or chicken, a sharing of the surplus of rural life. These redistributive relationships are expressions of ubuntu, referred to earlier. They illustrate the sense of solidarity and mutual obligation that binds people to one another.

There is often pressure on those living in the city to become in some sense patrons to the rural communities from which they have come. The pressure is towards a relationship where those in the village obtain some form of access to the resources of the city. In return, whether this is sought or not, the urban dweller obtains increased status in his village and rural community.

The social and economic structure of Luke's world however was largely built around patron-client relationships, social relationships between individuals based on a strong element of inequality and difference in power (Moxnes, 1991, pp. 241–268). A patron would be in possession of social, economic, and political resources that were needed by a client and so the client showed loyalty and respect to a patron in the hope of gaining greater access to those resources.

Within Luke's Gospel, we see a society divided between center and periphery, city and village, between Jerusalem and the outlying regions (Moxnes, 1991, p. 252). Patterns of patronage often followed these fault lines. The social and economic gaps they represented were vast and therefore there existed brokers whose role was to bridge the gap between those at the very centers of power and those at the margins. Following Chambers's (1997) line of thought, these brokers were lowers to the urban elite at the very center of power and uppers to those at the periphery.

In Luke 7, we meet the Roman centurion, who represents the outside military and administrative power, but who has become a patron to the community through such acts as building a synagogue. The parable of the dishonest steward (Luke 16:1–9) is also constructed around these relationships of center and margin with a broker acting between them, in this instance the steward. In writing down the debts, the steward uses his economic opportunity to establish a patron-client relationship with those who were in debt to the master. A similar picture of a broker relationship is seen with the nobleman in Luke 19 who, in going to a far-off land, leaves servants to manage his interests. These servants were effectively brokers, stewards of his wealth, whose right stewardship was later rewarded with gifts of cities (Moxnes, 1991).

As we will see in the next chapter, the rich of Luke's Gospel are not presented to us as beneficiaries of the communities in which they are in economic relationship. The relationship is not one marked by the degrees of reciprocity found in rural communities. Their patronage is selfish and based around greed and the hoarding of resources. While the rural poor may look to these relationships for generosity, Jesus's parables of the rich fool and the rich man and Lazarus, speak instead of an elite out of touch with the poor. The poor of the land, we see in

Luke, should expect nothing either from the rich elites or the brokers who serve as religious and community leaders.

Patrons as Brokers of Religion

This relationship of center to periphery and patron to client, with the broker as an intermediary, is not limited to the world of business and agriculture. Critically, Moxnes notes the role of religion in this dynamic. The role of scribes, Pharisees, and heads of the synagogues was to act as brokers facilitating access to the Torah, the Temple, and ultimately to God. Yet instead of performing that role, they become an obstruction. In Luke 14, the Pharisees are portrayed as those who fail to share tables with the poor and whose legalism would obstruct a crippled man from being healed. While they claim to be benefactors of the community, in reality their lives are described as being marked by greed and extortion (Moxnes, 1991, p. 256).

Into this world of patron and client, Luke presents us with a picture of Jesus who represents the transformation of these distorted social, economic, and religious relationships. First, we see that Jesus constantly moves between these worlds of center and periphery, village and city. He combines them in his own person. He locates himself at the very margins of society, yet will also address the elite of his day. He moves from Galilee to Jerusalem. He is not the broker who takes the traditional role of representing the will of the patron to the client. Instead, he identifies with those at the very margins. When, in Luke 14, he urges the Pharisees to invite to their tables those who can never pay them back, he undermines the very root of patronage, where giving and hospitality can no longer be used to create clients (Moxnes, 1991, p. 264).

Yet Jesus's role as broker is not only confined to this social mediation. Within Luke, God is the great benefactor, the only true benefactor, and Christ is the broker. In miracles and healing, Jesus makes available the resources of the Father in the name of the Father (Moxnes, 1991, p. 258). The relationship built on power, dominance, and exploitation is reconfigured to one built around generosity and grace and one that is directed first to the weak and lowly while the rich are sent away empty-handed.

Chapter 4
Making Some Early Connections: Luke's Context and Ours

My humanity is bound up in yours, for we can only be human together.

--Desmond Tutu

We have already noted the dangers of uncritically moving between the world that forms the background to Luke's Gospel and the world of our day. This is even more the case in the discussion of cities whose nature, size, and complexity are far removed from the streets and thoroughfares of the Jerusalem of Jesus's day. Yet there are themes that even now we can consider before we move further into Luke's Gospel.

Friendship at the Margins

We already have noted that Luke places Jesus in a world, both rural and urban, which is marked by profound division. It is a world occupied by the insider and the outsider. We see Jesus moving in the liminal places, locating himself among the social margins of his day even as he communicates the good news of the Kingdom to those who occupy the central ground. In parables, these divisions of insider and outsider seem to be constantly questioned, undermining the sense that those at the social, cultural, or even religious center form the center of God's Kingdom. In fact, often the reverse is true, and the margins where Jesus, "the friend of sinners" (Luke 7:34)—a designation not intended a compliment—so often locates himself are central and not peripheral to the Kingdom of God.

Drawing particularly from Mark's Gospel, Costas (1989) interprets Jesus's location in Galilee not as a historical accident, but as a purposeful identification with a marginalized community. For Costas, "Galilee of the Gentiles" reflects the social, political, economic, and religious margins of society. He argues that Galilee is normative for our understanding of mission and evangelism as a movement from the margins to the center. Evangelization, he argues, should be informed by the Galilee context—the context of the margins. The base of evangelism is an association with the lowest level, the most poor and marginalized in society (p. 62).

It is among those who have come into conflict with the norms and values of the community, by illness, poverty, or their own actions that Jesus so often locates himself. As we saw in Luke 14, it is those who in their poverty and exclusion are compelled to live at the periphery of the city, outside the city walls, who find themselves invited to the feast of the Kingdom. While the Pharisees pursued an agenda that sought to distance and protect themselves from those who threatened their own purity and that of the communities they led, Jesus disputed and challenged these boundaries in his lifestyle, relationships, and teaching (Moxnes, 1988, p. 55).

It is not difficult to identify those who in our day exist as social and cultural outsiders. Social stigma and stigma associated with disease, lifestyle, or abject poverty have not miraculously disappeared. Yet sadly, in the church, it often seems we have tended to follow the path of the Pharisees. We consider erecting boundaries for the preservation of certain notions of holiness and purity as more important than standing with those at the margins of our cultural, social, or economic life. We love the idea that the sinless Jesus was the friend of sinners, but we choose our own friendship groups rather differently.

The church my family joined during our time in Cape Town is trying to develop models of ministry that create spaces in which new forms of friendship and hospitality can be expressed and that seek to bridge deeply rooted divisions. It hosts a simple weekly meal that both congregation members and people living on the street can share together. It is radically different from a soup kitchen, because it is built around the idea of a shared table. It is hospitality, not distribution. Its strength is best experienced when as a newcomer I was not altogether clear who was from the church, who was from the street, and who belonged to both!

Yet even in something so intentionally rooted in hospitality, I see the default positions emerging, certainly in myself and perhaps in others. I quickly learned that service of those at the margins is far easier to implement than friendship. For churches committed to engaging with those at the margins of their neighborhoods, it becomes easy to move into positions built on yet another form of patron-client relationship, this time becoming service providers, and increasingly, professional helpers. Fundamentally, the Gospel calls us into friendships that overcome the barriers that so quickly emerge between us. Yet patterns of relationship, elite and nonelite, the insider and the outsider, those within the walls and those without, will constantly try to re-assert themselves as normative patterns. I quickly discovered that waiting on tables and washing up, being active and useful, was far less demanding and superficially more rewarding than sitting and forming friendships with those whose nights were spent on pavements and subways. Jesus was profoundly criticized for those he ate with and the company he kept. It is seldom a criticism leveled at those of us in church leadership, and when it is, it is generally not the poor in our company who attract the attention.

Forgiving Debt

Through Luke's eyes, we see Jesus entering a world of social and economic crisis. It is a world dominated by an empire and its emissaries in which vast sections of society feel oppressed and disempowered. This sense of economic oppression is marked by relationships of inequality, of servant to master, landlord to tenant, day laborer to employer, distorted patron-client relationships. Practically it is evidenced in the reality of unpayable debt. While in Luke's Gospel these realities are played out in parables often located in the small details of rural life, it is not difficult to see some aspects of them played out in our day. We see it on the macro stage of the global economy, of national debts, and of distorted trade relationships engineered around the seemingly endless supply of cheap labor. We see it in the realities of life in our own streets and cities. We see it in the crisis of the unpayable loan, whether at national levels or in the households that run to Wonga, the loan shark, or the credit company but find themselves in a downward spiral of ever-increasing debt.

In the late 1990s, I joined with thousands of others in forming a human chain around the center of the city of Birmingham. It was all part of the Jubilee campaign for the breaking of the chains of unpayable debt demanded of Heavily Indebted Poor Countries (HIPIC). It was part of a movement that evolved into the Make Poverty History campaign. The idea of making poverty history seemed a great ideal until I was challenged by a Kenyan colleague. Gently, he asked me the searching questions I had never heard raised by anyone in the United Kingdom. Why do you want to make poverty history? Why is your emphasis on ending poverty rather than ending greed that lies at the root of poverty? Why do you make others, their poverty, rather than yourselves, your greed, central to this problem? If the campaign were against greed—personal, corporate, and national—would you join hands with such enthusiasm?

Urging governments to act justly in relation to issues such as sovereign debt has undeniably had a positive impact on many nations in the developing world. But there remains the fundamental question of whether each of us would be equally active in addressing levels of global poverty if it demanded a significant scaling down of our lifestyles and choices. We cannot naively assume that lifting large numbers of people out of poverty can be achieved without some alteration and cost in terms of our own lifestyles. Patterns of consumption, enjoyed by most of us in the developed world, are simply unsustainable on a global scale. For many of us, our use of the earth's resources would be economically and environmentally unsustainable if they were enjoyed at the same level by the world's poor. If I want to see significant change in the lives of the world's poor, I may have to confront the possibility that the problem lies not only in the circumstances of their lives and experiences but in mine also. When I recognize that reality, the question for some of us of what constitutes an authentic and responsible Christian lifestyle becomes ever more urgent.

In Luke, we see this authentic response rooted in the way we pray. We have seen how the Lord's Prayer touches on the very issues of debt and debt forgiveness. This prayer of Jesus is recited by Christians all around the world. It can be heard in the most ornate cathedrals, vast megachurches, tin-shack churches, barrios, *favelas*, or informal settlements of the urban poor. It is a prayer said to unite Christians around the world, and yet its words are lost on many of us in its comfortable familiarity.

Shane Claiborne (2006), one of the founding members of The Simple Way, a faith community in Philadelphia, tellingly observes the way the rather obscure prayer of Jabez, with its individualistic hope of enlarging his territory, seems to resonate more easily with American Christians than Jesus's corporate prayer for our daily bread (p. 318). I have found it helpful to try to make it part of my daily discipline in praying the Lord's Prayer to hold before God, in the expression of daily bread, the hungry and the homeless of God's world. The prayer offers a moment of solidarity to stand prayerfully with those who cry for bread for today. When I do that, the prayer moves from something directed to my personal needs to a sense of being in solidarity with God's wider family. We speak of the Lord's Prayer as the family prayer of the church, yet we need to let it remind us that our family includes the poor and hungry of the earth, whose daily longing is for something as basic as bread. Prayer then moves us to exploring what it means to live in the midst of those realities and how to seek the things we pray for.

Just as Christ's prayer for our daily bread can challenge our personal response to the hungry, so his teaching on debt will encourage us to think of our practice in lending. Lending is generally calculated around the likelihood of items being returned or payments refunded. Do we refuse to lend when a previous loan was not repaid, even when we see the need persisting?

An emphasis on debt repayment over debt forgiveness makes a virtue of expediency, owing more to the logic of economic systems than the logic of the Kingdom. It is also a view of the world seen from the perspective of the lender. Yet as we will constantly see in Luke, we are invited to encounter the world from another perspective. In the crippling economic climate of his day, Jesus encouraged his followers not to restrict what they can lend only to those who will most likely repay. Applying lending restrictions would have made good economic sense but would probably result in not lending to the most economically disadvantaged or to those whose economic plight was chronic rather than temporary. It is those in similar positions today who find themselves driven towards borrowing at extortionate levels of interest because other channels are not open to them.

We may fear the impact of unpaid debts on our relationship with the debtor, and yet such situations can in reality be avenues for gift and grace. In contexts of great economic disparity, which has the greater moral imperative, the debtor to repay or the lender to forgive? I suspect we usually stress the former, yet to those would-be followers of Jesus the answer is the reverse. His words may seem impractical and difficult, but they are also liberating when we find ourselves more deeply concerned with the one to whom something was lent than with the item or sum that was lent.

Addressing the Walls

> *There is a green hill far away*
> *Without a city wall*
> *Where the dear Lord was crucified*
> *Who died to save us all.*
> Cecil Frances Alexander, "There Is a Green Hill Far Away"

Like many children who grew up going to Sunday school, I have memories of creating Easter gardens that appeared at the back of church during Holy Week leading to Good Friday and Easter. Made from papier-mâché or strips of artificial grass, these models had a number of things in common. There would be the green hill with the three crosses placed on it, with Jesus prominently in the center. Some distance away would be a lesser mound housing a small cave, with a stone just to one side of it. Being British, the whole scene around the tomb was decorated with the brilliant spring colors lent by daffodils and primroses.

I suspect that many of these much-loved representations of the site of the passion and resurrection of Jesus owe rather more to the poetry and imagination of the hymn writer Cecil Frances Alexander than to the realities of first-century Jerusalem. "Outside the city wall" creates, for some of us, images of idyllic rolling hills and gardens. In reality, outside the city wall speaks far more profoundly of a place outside the order and security of urban life. Outside the city walls is the province of those excluded, the destitute and dispossessed, pushed even from the very margins of life inside the city. Such places included Gehenna, Jerusalem's ever-smoking rubbish dump, and Golgotha, the place of the skull and of crucifixion.

To be outside the city wall, therefore, can take on the meaning of somehow being outside the "good" of the city. It can mean existing beyond the reaches of the city's benefits, protection, community. In medieval times, as we saw in the concept of banns, it had the sense of being outside the civilization of urban life. This is unprotected, undervalued space.

Although city walls became irrelevant in the vast urban growth of the industrial era, they remain in urban landscapes in forms less immediately apparent but no less real. Life outside the city wall, outside the rights, opportunities, and benefits of urban life is experienced in cities on every continent—in decaying tenements, on city center pavements, under railway arches, and in informal settlement communities on the physical fringes of cities in the developing world.

Sometimes it appears as if the city wall that once existed as a boundary and protection for the community of the city has been radically privatized. The walls of today's cities no longer surround entire communities but more often protect privileged islands of private space in gated communities, suburban estates, and citadel-like office complexes (Hollis, 2013, p. 161). This championing of the security of the individual and of private space above the wider public good is particularly evident in the global growth of the private security industry. In South Africa, it is a 30 billion Rand industry, with the number of private security officers exceeding that of the police force (South African Catholic Bishops' Conference, 2011, p. 1). Meanwhile, a city such as London is protected by more than half a million security cameras, such that the casual walker through the city is likely to be caught on camera more than 300 times in a day (Hollis, 2013, p. 166). In what writer Mike Davis (1992) refers to as the "militarization of urban space," cities risk becoming places marked by ever-diminishing levels of trust and by the desire to retain and protect against the fear of the unknown other. For some however, whose lives are often lived amongst the "unknown other," city life offers little that might be protected or preserved.

Elizabeth lives in Korogocho, one of Nairobi's informal settlements. When I met her, she was facing the heavily polluted

Nairobi River while looking toward the seemingly endless horizon of Dandora dumpsite. In this modern day Gehenna, the vast bulk of Nairobi's refuse is deposited by a constant convoy of trucks. Yet here is also the place where hundreds of others make their hazardous living scavenging for recyclables to sell to more affluent middlemen.

On her back, Elizabeth carried her youngest child while another stood quietly at her side. Below her, up to their waists in the river, were two other daughters. Together they were cleaning polythene bags collected from the dumpsite while further away two other children dried them on the grass. If she and her children could wash and clean 500 bags in a day, there would be a sufficient income for food and rent, but nothing with which to send the children to school. She had migrated into the city following the breakup of her marriage and was trying to survive with the help of an older sister who had made the same journey before her. They lived, precariously, at the social and economic margins of the city.

Nairobi, like virtually all modern cities, does not have a city wall. But for hundreds of thousands of people like Elizabeth, their lives are lived outside the good, the welfare, and the protection of the city. They are in every other sense outside the city wall. Yet as Alexander's hymn reminds us, this place without meaning outside the wall is paradoxically the place of redemption. Here we encounter the crucified and risen Christ. "Outside the camp," where those excluded are to be found, is also the place of Christ (Selby, 1991, p. 58). Jesus was crucified outside the wall of the city, in the places of the destitute and the dispossessed. Many to this day find themselves exiled to similar places. Whatever mission means in this context, it must require us to recover a sense that the sources of grace and transformation are not to be located in centers of power and privilege but rather at the margins, outside the wall, in the places we call Golgotha. For in the words of Father Alex Zanotelli, who I quoted in the introduction, "If God exists, he can only be found in Korogocho."

Envisioning a City Without Walls

What then might it mean to live in a city without walls where boundaries of inclusion and exclusion give way to create new and as yet unrealized expressions of hospitality and community? The question is by no means a novel one. The prophet Zechariah envisioned such a possibility centuries earlier. In his vision, we see the city of Jerusalem is reimagined as an unwalled city: "Jerusalem shall be inhabited as villages without walls, because of the multitude of people and livestock in it" (Zech. 2:4). The scene is one of such overflowing prosperity that walls cannot contain its people and livestock. To construct a wall would be to place a barrier that sets limits on the abundance of God's intention for the city. Paradoxically, while protection of wealth and prosperity are so often the driving force behind the construction of walls, in Zechariah's vision it is abundance that makes the walls obsolete.

The city without walls becomes the image of a flourishing city, which is radically open to those who are not yet its inhabitants. Critically, the vision is directed to God's people who have remained in Babylonian exile. The call is to return to a city whose walls will not keep them out. But this is not the unprotected city. Yahweh is to be the wall of fire around her. This is the faithful city, where Yahweh is the glory in her midst (Zech. 2:5). This is the city whose communal and corporate life reveals the glory of God, whose security is rooted in trust, and whose borders are ever open to include those who are spread abroad. Neither is the picture restricted to the people of Israel, for in this city God's glory will be revealed among the nations (Zech 2:11).

In Zechariah's vision, we catch a glimpse of a truly global, faithful city that is a magnet to the nations. It is a city that enjoys prosperity without the signs and apparatus of security. It is a city where God's glory is joyously revealed in the midst of the nations. Even as we begin to look at the gaps and divisions of our urban world, we need to allow such dreaming to give prophetic substance to our own envisioning of urban life.

Transforming Structures of Relationship

Our discussion of patron-client relationships will describe scenarios that may seem alien to some readers yet very familiar to others. In modern societies with centralized government and bureaucratic systems, it can be difficult to envisage the way patron-client relationships work. In many societies, citizens expect to have equal access to certain public goods, and there are often laws designed to prevent discrimination in accessing them. This is not to deny the reality that in many so-called developed societies there remains profound inequality in access to public services. However, in a bureaucratic system, relationships are largely irrelevant. Of course, that system may be subverted. The old boys' network may assist in getting someone a job, but generally it won't get a hospital bed, speed up an unemployment benefit claim, or help obtain a tax or social security number.

In many traditional societies, certainly in parts of Africa, reciprocal and patron-client relationships continue and are linked to rural-urban relationships. Inequality in these relationships can be sustained and preserved by political and economic elites, who provide sufficient access to resources to sustain certain bonds but never sufficient to make them unnecessary. In other words, individuals and communities can be held in a relationship of constant dependency, where the benefits of loyalty are constantly promised but seldom realized and where the advantages of the relationship are firmly on the side of the patron. Patronage politics remains a reality (G. Myers & M. Murray, 2006, p. 18).

This negative form of patronage can be present at all levels. In examining the role patronage plays in providing access to education in Nigeria, researchers found that the structures of patronage preserved rather than reduced inequality. They concluded that patron-client relationships in their context produced an additional level of inequality that carried through generations (Morgan, Ismaila, & Salisu, 2010, pp. 79–103).

That such relationships can be exploitative and unjust is evident, both in Luke and in many societies where patronage remains embedded in political and economic life. As we have seen however, many rural urban migrants in cities like Nairobi will depend far more effectively on reciprocal-type relationships than on any government provision. The person from the village who has done well in the city, even if doing well is simply the ability to sustain himself or herself, will be expected to take on a reciprocal role to others moving in from the village. The extent of what is expected from the relationship varies between communities, but it is a present reality and an essential survival mechanism for many rural to urban migrants around the world.

However, what Luke suggests to us is the transformation of patronage, where the power imbalance in the relationship is totally removed. We are urged to give without asking for anything in return, to lend without the expectation of repayment, and to extend hospitality to those who will never be able to repay. The whole transactional basis of patronage is removed. The idea of a face-to-face, redistributive relationship that creates space for avenues of justice and generosity is preserved, but it is rooted entirely in mirroring God's beneficent action toward the poor rather than in creating those structures of status, power, and dependency that can so easily be evidenced in many mission and development programs among the urban poor.

Chapter 5
Wealth and Poverty in Luke's Gospel

Come all you vagabonds,
Come all you "don't belongs"
Winners and losers,
Come, people like me.

--Stuart Townend, "Vagabonds"

Uncomfortable Words

The parable of the rich man and Lazarus is probably not a favourite among preachers for obvious reasons. One person, however, who apparently didn't shy away from it was John Wesley. I think we can also be sure he did not soften its message in order not to offend his audience. In his journals, he refers to the parable at least four times. On one occasion, held up by bad weather, he finds himself preaching, to his surprise, "to a room full of men and women, daubed with gold and silver." Sensing they may be far from the Gospel, he selected his text carefully, "that I might not go out of their depth, I began by expounding the story of Dives and Lazarus." He notes sadly, "I delivered my soul, but they could in no wise bear it. One and another walked away, murmuring sorely" (April 29, 1750).

Much of my childhood was spent in a coal mining town in Yorkshire. There in the local parish church, where my father was the vicar, I committed my life to Christ. There, in a building where Christians had worshiped for almost a thousand years, I would sing in the church choir at choral evensong. Week by week we would join in the Magnificat from the Book of Common Prayer, singing the praises of a God who appears to have a habit of repeatedly upsetting unjust political and economic systems:

> He hath put down the mighty from their seat:
> and hath exalted the humble and meek.
> He hath filled the hungry with good things:
> and the rich he hath sent empty away.
> (Luke 1:52–53)

In all the years of singing those words, I confess it never occurred to me I might be celebrating a different kind of social order, which would profoundly challenge the world as I knew it. I suspect some would be horrified if they thought that commitment to such an idea was ever implied in the singing of the song! I later preached on the Magnificat in our local church in Kibera. It was one of those moments where you quickly discover that the congregation has grasped the essence of a passage more deeply and more authentically than the preacher. I found myself being taught by those who, from their place in history, can hear the words more clearly than I can.

When I read of the God who fills the hungry and lifts up the humble and of the dethroning of the proud while the rich are sent away empty-handed, some cheered while others laughed. For this congregation, gathered in an iron-sheet church in the heart of Kibera, it was as if their side had just won. God was on their side. This was not simply an affirmation of what God has done through history, but a celebration that God was for them. Their story was being told and heard and affirmed and a different future anticipated. I have preached on the same passage in the United Kingdom, but not with the same effect.

A second experience touches on the way we can edit the parts of Scripture that we find most difficult. There is a section in the Anglican liturgy that comes before a general confession. It is called the "comfortable words" and reminds us of a God who brings strength (the root meaning of the word comfort), assurance, and forgiveness. But occasionally I wonder whether we should have a section called the "uncomfortable words"—the words that disturb our comfort, shock us in our complacency, and challenge us to reimagine our lives in the light of Christ's call to a radical discipleship. Of course those words are there. We have seen them in the Magnificat. However, their familiarity seems to neutralize their impact.

Sometimes, however, we can unintentionally edit words out of the text, perhaps because we don't know what to do with them or they don't fit the message we intend to communicate. On one occasion, I was taking part in a conference in Johannesburg. It was a wonderful event that concluded with a sermon based on the words of Luke 12:32, "Do not be afraid, little flock, for your Father has been pleased to give you the Kingdom." The preacher delivered a very encouraging message. However, no reference was ever made of the words that immediately follow Jesus's statement and are surely inextricably linked to his promise. Luke 12:32–34 says:

> Sell your possessions and give to the poor. Provide purses for yourselves that will not wear out, a treasure in heaven that will not fail, where no thief comes and no moth destroys. For where your treasure is, there will your heart be also.

The treasures of the Kingdom seem to be closely tied to the use and sharing of material wealth. If there is a liturgy of "uncomfortable words," I suspect these verses would be part of them. We cannot pretend these are easy words to apply to our lives, but we may be building houses on shifting sand if we fail to consider what it means to respond to them with faith and obedience. That response may not result in something as radical and literal as that of St. Francis, who renounced all and stood naked in the presence of God, but we do have to consider what it means in our present situations to follow Jesus in the light of his teaching on wealth and poverty.

A Gospel for the Poor

Luke's Gospel is widely noted for the way it portrays Jesus's concern for the poor and the marginalized. Even before his birth, Mary is able to celebrate the reversed positions that will be realized in the advent of her son. In Jesus, rulers will be brought down from their thrones and the humble will be uplifted. The Lazaruses of this world will be filled with good things, while the rich will be sent away hungry (Luke 1:52–53).

As Jesus begins his ministry, in the so-called "Nazareth manifesto" he sets out his agenda for what lies ahead which, in prophetic fulfillment, will be good news to the poor (Luke 4:18–19). Quoting from Isaiah 61, Jesus declares Israel's messianic hope is being fulfilled here and now in their very hearing. These ancient words of hope will be realized in his very person, and experienced by the poor, the prisoner, the blind, and the oppressed.

As we have noted previously, this declaration needs to be understood against a context of poverty, debt, and imperial oppression. It must be understood as being proclaimed in "Galilee of the Gentiles" at the margins of the nation's political, economic, and religious life. These prophetic words were first addressed, in the book of Isaiah, to a city in crisis, to those who grieve in Zion (Isa 61:3), longing for restoration. In Luke, they are addressed to a rural community impoverished by the greed of an urban elite, who owe their privilege and allegiance to imperial Rome.

Jesus's use of the text may be more radical than it first appears. The passage, celebrating God's Jubilee, the year of Yahweh's favour, goes on to promise Israel will feed on the wealth of nations and boast in their riches (Isa 61:6). This is a dramatic reversal of his original listeners' present reality. While their experience is of tribute and taxation from Israel's poor to the central powers of the empire, what is promised is a new community, reflecting God's intention of justice for all the nations. Wealth will not flow from periphery to center but be redistributed among the nations (D. Smith, 2011).

These words of Jesus at Nazareth are echoed in Luke 7. John the Baptist, imprisoned by Herod Antipas, sends word to enquire through his disciples whether the one he baptized in the river Jordan is truly the anticipated Messiah, the one who is to come. If John expected Jesus to institute a messianic kingdom he could be forgiven for wondering why corrupt leaders remained in power while he, John, languished in prison. Where is the liberating Messiah?

Jesus's reply identifies his messianic credentials as being exhibited in the lives of the blind, the lame, the unclean, the deaf, and in those raised from death to life. The evidence presented to John, that Jesus is truly God's anointed and that he is "the one," is that good news is preached to the poor (Luke 7:22). The Gospel is made real in the lives of those at the very margins of society.

In Luke's account of the Sermon on the Plain, it is the materially poor who inherit God's Kingdom. It is those like Lazarus at the gate, those who are literally hungry now, who will be satisfied (Luke 6:21). We see here the way the good news of the Kingdom is presented as breaking into the realities of their lives. It is not a kingdom that can only be anticipated in a distant future or over the horizon in another world yet to come. In Luke, we see the coming of the Kingdom of God in the person of Jesus of Nazareth. In Jesus, the eschatological reversal, the great reversal that will take place in the kingdom that is to come, has already begun. In him, the hungry are being filled with good things, and the rich are being sent empty away.

This theme of a concern for the poor continues throughout the Gospel. We have observed that Jesus instructs his disciples to sell all they have and give to the poor (Luke 12:33) and to renounce all they have (Luke 14:33). It presents a challenge to discipleship that the rich ruler sadly cannot attain (Luke 18:23).

This radical vulnerability is evident in the sending out of the 12 (Luke 9: 1–9) and the 72 (Luke 10:1–16). In each case, they are sent without money or material resources, dependent on the generosity of the poor and the provision of the Lord of the harvest. Ultimately it will be the blind beggar by the road who will follow Jesus (Luke 18:43) and Zacchaeus, the despised tax collector, who embodies true discipleship and genuine repentance as he shares his wealth with the poor (Luke 19:8). These appear in Luke to be among the pointers to what it means to be inheritors of the Kingdom.

"Good News" for the Rich?

We have noted Luke's concern for the poor, yet there is also, expressed very differently, a concern for the rich. As we saw in Chapter 2, it is the eternal welfare of the rich in his community that may have been a primary concern for Luke (Kuhn, 2010, p. 105). There is no indication in the Gospel that wealth in and of itself leads a person on the path to hell or that poverty in itself reaps a reward in paradise (Jeremias, 1972). However, wealth is often expressed as a stumbling block to entering the Kingdom rather than as a sign of God's blessing.

Throughout Luke's travel narrative (Luke 9:51–19:27), Metzger observed that a number of the parables contain common features associated with wealth. They have similar characters (wealthy men), similar settings (elite residences), and a common motif (overconsumption) (Metzger, as cited by Moore, 2011, p. 202). These features are most graphically illustrated in the parable of the rich man and Lazarus, but they do present a recurring theme in this section of the Gospel.

Within these parables, we see warnings about a demonic form of mammon that takes hold of people and enslaves them, often with eternal consequences (Moxnes, 1988, p. 150). They are subversive stories, fundamentally challenging listeners to reorder and remold the cultural and economic reality around them (Arbuckle, 2010, p. 163). The hearers are faced with critical choices about what or who exercises authority over their lives. There appears no room for compromise, no possibility of serving two masters (Luke 16:13). Wealth can either be used faithfully, in service of God and so in solidarity with or on behalf of those in need, or it can take a demonic hold of our lives, becoming a master in this life and shaping our eternal destiny (Green, 1997, p. 596).

In Luke 12:16, we encounter a successful farmer who has experienced a bumper harvest. Yet his great fortune is swiftly turned to disaster as he plots to pull down barns and create something bigger and better through which he will ensure for himself a future life of comfort where he can eat, drink, and be merry. This selfish hoarding of wealth results in the judgment, "You fool! This very night your life will be demanded from you" (Luke 12:20). The rhetorical question, "Then who will get what you have prepared for yourself?" only serves to underline the way the farmer has planned his future with no thought for anyone other than himself. At the point when the most appropriate response would have been thankfulness to the Lord of the Harvest, we find the words "And I will say to myself" (Luke 12:19). Reminiscent of the Pharisee of Luke 18, who prays to or about himself, this rich man's self-centeredness is his downfall.

The rich man comes to the point where he defines the good life in ways that are allergic to true wisdom. In words that have a profound relevance for our own age, Michael Moore (2011) comments, "Thus his unwillingness to deal with the crisis of his prosperity, and it is a crisis, ultimately leads him to make the decision to equate his life with his possessions" (p. 210).

Like the people of Israel who sought to preserve manna over the eve of the Sabbath, only to see it destroyed by maggots, so the self-centered farmer loses his crop. But not only his crop—his life as well. Whether it is the selfishness of the hoarding farmer, the conspicuous consumption of the rich man in Luke 16, or the neglect of the Pharisee to share his table with the poor (Luke 14:12–14), we see that money and wealth, become in these hands "unrighteous mammon" and take on a new dimension, in direct opposition to God (Talbert, 1984, p. 146).

The use of wealth in Luke's Gospel is most frequently illustrated in the most obvious way the people could redistribute their wealth—through hospitality and the sharing of food. An appropriate response of a farmer with a bumper crop would have been to hold a feast in which all the village could share in his prosperity and the fertility of the land on which they too would have worked. Instead, he hoards it. From Luke 14 through Luke 15 we see a recurrent theme of feasts, parties, and banquets where joy is celebrated and relationships are restored or where selfishness and greed excludes others from the table.

An Awkward Dinner Party

The parable of the banquet comes in the middle of a rather awkward dinner party in which Jesus demonstrates his capacity to be anything but the perfect guest. Whatever the poor host's equivalent was of a Christmas card list, you can be pretty sure Jesus wasn't going to be on it, and that this outing into religious high society was unlikely to elicit repeat invitations from the other guests. Luke tells us Jesus was being carefully watched (Luke 14:2). That day he certainly gave them something to see!

Jesus begins a series of what appear to be social gaffes by healing a sick man on the Sabbath in the Pharisee's own home and then challenging the assembled Pharisees and legal experts on the legitimacy of his action. The guests observe a discreet silence so, undeterred, Jesus, observing the way they have all been competing for the best seat at the table, launches into a story about social climbing. The poor host has barely recovered from this caustic assessment of his guests' table manners when Jesus attacks the host himself and the socially exclusive nature of the dinner party. It has been restricted to all his deeply religious colleagues and likeminded friends and relations. Jesus points out that for a real party, you need the poor, the crippled (like the man with dropsy, the uninvited guest whom Jesus releases from the party), the blind, the lame, and anyone you can think of who couldn't possibly invite you back to their place. Bring them together and you really have a feast, a party, a genuinely great banquet. He slips in at the end that they will be repaid at the resurrection of the righteous, providing the link into the theme of heavenly banquets.

In the midst of this social embarrassment, one of the guests tries to turn the conversation onto safer ground. Hearing the words "resurrection of the righteous," he makes the pious declaration, "Blessed is the man who will eat at the feast in the Kingdom of God" (Luke 14:15). My suspicion at this point is that he anticipates those who will eat at this feast in the age to come are pretty much the same sort of people as those currently seated at the table. If so, he could not be further from the truth. If he was hoping to shift the conversation away from references to the poor, the crippled, the blind, and lame, then this was a disaster. The same characters the host has omitted from his meal table are the ones in the parable who are found to be seated at the great banquet Jesus describes.

Jesus turns the feast idea upside down. The poor, who have been excluded from the table where he has been sitting, are the ones who get to feast. Who then are the invited guests who will never get to taste even the crumbs that fall from the table? I suspect the host is praying in his heart of hearts that none of his esteemed guests asks the question. There is only so much humiliation you can take in your own home!

As we saw earlier, Jesus is subverting the whole patron-client relationship. The prominent Pharisee who has hosted the party has invited other Pharisees and religious experts (Luke 14:3) and possibly relatives and rich neighbors (Luke 14:12). As religious leaders, they are in some ways brokers between the people and the Torah, the Temple and, in some sense, God. Yet by both their attitudes and actions they have used religion as a means to exclude the crippled man, and fundamental to patron-client relationships, used wealth as a means to acquire and secure relationships among an economic elite.

The parable of the banquet centers on the rejection and the acceptance of God's invitation, revealed in the person of Jesus. In their rejection of Jesus, the guests reject the banquet he speaks of. Looking at the church Luke was addressing, the parable would have spoken of the way many in the Jewish nation rejected Jesus even as the Gospel went out to the highways and byways of the Gentile world (N.T. Wright, 2004, p. 178). However, we must not lose sight of the relationship of the parable to Jesus's words in Luke 14:12–14. We anticipate God's eternal banquet by extending his invitation to those at the social and economic margins. In case we miss the point, that is not simply about extending a welcome invitation to God's table, but also to our own.

A True Party

If Luke 16 contains one of Jesus's most neglected parables, the same cannot be said for Luke 15. This chapter contains what Robert Capon (1998) terms the Party Parables. Luke tells us that Jesus was teaching very mixed company that included Pharisees and sinners (Luke 15:1). The telling observation in verse two is that the Pharisees complained that Jesus welcomed sinners and ate with them. It is no accident therefore that the parables that follow each conclude with a party to which all are included. In each, the celebration points to the joy at the reconciliation of the sinner. While the first two parables do not indicate the problems some may have in sharing their table with those they deem less worthy, the parable of the lost son concludes with precisely that dilemma.

The ending of the parable of the lost son (Luke 15:11–32) centers on one who is included in the invitation and yet who finds himself out in the cold. In the end, the one who does not make it to the meal has excluded himself. He has built his own chasm, denied and separated himself from his brother (Luke 15:25–32). While the father, in the fellowship of the table, seeks to restore to the household and the village the son who is lost, the elder brother seeks to perpetuate his exclusion. Ironically, it is ultimately the elder brother who turns out to be the most lost by his refusal to celebrate with the father the return of his brother. This refusal to share at the table links this parable to the end of Luke 16 where it is the failure to share with Lazarus at the gate that has locked the rich man out of the heavenly banquet. Both, by their self-centeredness, have locked themselves outside the gate of the heavenly feast, excluding themselves by their exclusion of others.

The Parable of the Rich Man and Lazarus in the Context of Luke 16

The thread linking Luke 14 and 15 with Luke 16 is the Pharisees' criticism of Jesus for sharing his table with sinners and outcasts and Jesus's criticism of the Pharisees for not sharing their table with the poor and the outcast. Luke 16 focuses almost exclusively on the question of wealth, the economy of the Kingdom. Here wisdom in the use of worldly resources is applauded (Luke 16 1–12), and selfish and heartless use of wealth has eternal consequences.

The parables of the shrewd manager (Luke 16: 1–12) and the rich man and Lazarus (Luke 16: 19–31) share a common beginning, "There was a rich man." In the first parable, the emphasis turns out not to lie with the rich man but with his steward who is on the verge of losing his job. Having been found lazy or incompetent with his master's resources his future suddenly looks bleak, with little option beyond a life of hard labor or begging. In a moment of pure genius, he hits on a solution. He will discount all his master's debts. The debts are large, so these are substantial businesses. Gratified by his unauthorized, but apparently binding largesse, the debtors will be willing to offer him a job when his current master fires him.

The parable concludes with Jesus's words, "I tell you, use worldly wealth to gain friends for yourselves, so that when it is gone you will be welcomed into the eternal dwellings" (Luke 16:9). The verse reflects the words of the steward in Luke 16:4, "I know what I will do so that, when I lose my job here, people will welcome me into their houses." The steward plans to use the wealth at his disposal to establish relationships that will secure his earthly future. In Jesus's comment in verse 9 however, wealth is not to be seen as establishing and securing earthly relationships, something he has already condemned (Luke 14:12–14). Rather, worldly wealth should be used to gain friends who will secure you a welcome into eternal dwellings.

Of course, we have to ask at this point: "Who are these friends who secure a welcome into the heavenly dwelling?" The answer should have been found on the lips of the rich fools of chapters 12 and 16. Lazarus, it would appear, had the key to the rich man's destiny; friendship with Lazarus would, one suspects, have left the rich man in a very different predicament. Likewise, the greedy farmer whose response to the Lord of the Harvest is to build bigger silos to hoard ever-greater wealth might have heard a different voice in the night if he had shared his blessing with his neighbors. Making friends by means of unrighteous mammon, sharing with the poor, turns out to have eternal consequences.

Luke is developing a simple equation for us. Faithfulness with worldly wealth (read: sharing your bread with the poor) and unfaithfulness with worldly wealth (read: hoarding, conspicuous consumption, a disregard for the poor, i.e. living under the rule of mammon) have eternal consequences. These consequences are spelled out for us in the parable of the rich man and Lazarus.

Chapter 6
The Story with a Hole in It

His was always a story with a hole in it: a wrong story,
always wrong.

--J.M. Coetzee, *The Life and Times of Michael K*

J.M. Coetzee's Man Booker prizewinning novel, *The Life and Times
of Michael K*, tells the story of a South African man who is caught up in
the midst of a war he cannot comprehend. At one point in the novel,
the main character, Michael, finds himself in what is described as a
resettlement camp. In reality, it is a dumping ground for the growing
ranks of the poor and destitute. There he meets Robert, a man who
seeks to preserve his dignity and independence amid his and his
family's struggle for survival. He is deeply cynical about those who seem
to demonstrate some compassion in a system lacking in humanity. In
one telling conversation about those who appeared to offer some
improvement to their insanitary conditions, Robert questions Michael's
naïveté about their motives and intentions:

> Do you think they do it because they love us? Not a hope.
> They prefer it that we live because we look too terrible
> when we get sick and die. If we just grew thin and turned
> into paper and then into ash and then floated away, they
> wouldn't give a stuff for us. They just don't want to get
> upset. They want to go to sleep feeling good.

In the same conversation, Robert tells Michael to look into their hearts and wake up to the truth around him.

The dialogue makes uncomfortable reading. It disturbs us in at least two levels. First, the clear distinctions we want to make between the good guys and the bad guys in an unjust system are blurred or even denied. Those whose actions seem to be ameliorating injustice are merely disguising it beneath a superficial coating of care. Second, motives are questioned and found wanting.

Do you think they do it because they love us? Coetzee asks a profound question with an unfashionable turn of phrase. Television appeals, advertisements, and junk mail constantly urge people to respond to any number of global crises: an earthquake in Haiti, a tsunami in the Pacific, a flood in Malawi, or a famine in Ethiopia. The publicity goes out urging people to respond to the images of need, suffering, and hardship. But what is being appealed to? What moves people to give?

In the midst of these appeals, there are levels of cynicism on both sides of the equation. Cynicism is there among those who give. They wonder whether the funds reach the supposed targets and question why, after decades of aid, we seem to be no closer to addressing the problems of global poverty. Somehow we might sleep a little better if we knew we were. Those on the other side see aid and development as little more than another industry and wonder at the motivation of the governments, agencies, and individuals behind it. They see it as a process that, in the name of fundraising, exploits and often distorts and perverts their image. The efforts of international aid agencies are perceived as subsidizing poverty and disguising the structures of injustice that maintain cycles of crisis, which form the basis of so many appeals. Reflecting this perspective, the African economist and author of Dead Aid, Dambisa Moyo, has described aid as "the disease of which it pretends to be the cure" (as cited by Lupton, 2012, p. 3).

My purpose here is not to discuss the effectiveness or otherwise of international aid. It is certainly not to defend those who cynically exploit its weaknesses in order to obscure our shared responsibility to pursue justice and equity. If we may speak of a War on Terror, let it be a war on the terrors of injustice, greed, poverty, and preventable suffering and disease. Our issue here however is how we pursue those ends in ways that do not reduce others to "objects of our pity and patronage" (Lupton, 2012, p. 5).

Reflecting on Robert's words to Michael, it is easy to see how we can get locked into structures of relationships that distort the way we see each other and leave both parties diminished as a result. We seem unable to reach across the barriers constructed between us. What would make Robert believe in the integrity and humanity of those whose supposed help he despised? Could the helpers possibly reimagine themselves in a different role and relationship? Could they see themselves through Robert's eyes?

The earliest Christians were known for the way they loved one another. It was seen as the defining characteristic of the Christian community. For Robert it equally appears that the presence or absence of love was what validated or, in this case, invalidated expressions of help and assistance. Love in this context would not have been some emotional expression of concern. Written in the 1980s against the backdrop of apartheid, something more fundamental is implied in the book: a love that would radically transform their relationships and the injustices and inequalities that lay at the root of them.

In Luke 16 we are transported into a world that seems to hold up a mirror to the economic distortions of our day. In one of the most neglected parables of Jesus, we encounter a rich man and a poor beggar whose lives are physically close and yet radically far apart, to the point that they never meet or connect (Bailey, 2008, pp. 12–30). One is, to misquote the band U2, "Here without a name in the palace of his shame," while the other possesses nothing but his name, the only character in a parable of Jesus who is named.

The parable seems to lack all those nuanced discussions about the ways help, care, aid, or development are made available and the motivation behind them. There is no help or offer. Like Michael K's story, it too is "a wrong story, a story with a hole in it". More precisely, it is a story with a gap in it, a chasm that runs through the parable and, as we shall see, plays out in the structure of the storytelling. Yet it is a story with immense contemporary relevance that illustrates not only the realities of cities around the globe but also the significance of these chasms and divides in God's economy.

A World Turned Upside Down

In Luke 16:19–31, we read:

There was a rich man who was dressed in purple and fine linen and lived in luxury every day. At his gate was laid a beggar named Lazarus, covered with sores and longing to eat what fell from the rich man's table. Even the dogs came and licked his sores.

The time came when the beggar died and the angels carried him to Abraham's side. The rich man also died and was buried. In Hades, where he was in torment, he looked up and saw Abraham far away, with Lazarus by his side. So he called to him, "Father Abraham, have pity on me and send Lazarus to dip the tip of his finger in water and cool my tongue, because I am in agony in this fire."

But Abraham replied, "Son, remember that in your lifetime you received your good things, while Lazarus received bad things, but now he is comforted here and you are in agony. And besides all this, between us and you a great chasm has been fixed, so that those who want to go from here to you cannot, nor can anyone cross over from there to us."

He answered, "Then I beg you father, send Lazarus to my father's house, for I have five brothers. Let him warn them, so that they will not also come to this place of torment."

Abraham replied, "They have Moses and the Prophets; let them listen to them."

"No, father Abraham," he said, "but if someone from the dead goes to them they will repent."

He said to him, "If they do not listen to Moses and the Prophets, they will not be convinced even if someone rises from the dead."

Lazarus sits at the rich man's gate. Carried by the hopes and expectations of others he attends to his silent vigil. He is ministered to only by dogs, until his pitiful existence ceases and he is transported into the arms of Abraham. He and the rich man are the neighbors who never speak, their lives close enough to touch yet far enough apart for one to be rendered invisible by the other. They are the personifications of abundance and poverty, laid out in parallel lines, never to intersect in ways that might divert, even redeem, the course of history in the other.

In the brief cameo of their earthly lives, the rich man and Lazarus present us with the bleakest scenario of the gulfs that emerge between people. The physical gap between Lazarus at the gate and the rich man at his table points us towards the economic gap, portrayed in rags and purple linen, hunger and plenty. Most profoundly, the gulf of silence that hangs between them in life, and continues beyond the grave, points to a seemingly irreconcilable chasm of eternal consequence.

The parables of Jesus all seem to have one purpose in mind, to take the given truths and accepted wisdom of the day and turn it on its head. They reveal a kingdom that from almost every angle fails to conform to the image anticipated by the hearers. The parable of the rich man and Lazarus is no exception. Speaking into a worldview that sees wealth as a blessing from God and poverty as sign of divine disapproval, we discover a wealthy son of Abraham who finds himself in Hades, while a beggar is promoted to the highest and most revered place of all in the bosom of Abraham. For the Pharisees, who seem to be the intended initial audience, this was not a comfortable message. It represented a dramatic reversal of how they understood the blessings of a faithful life. But it also creates problems for the contemporary reader.

As we read the parable, it is not entirely clear what the rich man has done wrong or what Lazarus has done right to justify such a radical and permanent parting of their ways. Like the rich man of Luke 12:16–21, this man is not portrayed as having done anything morally wrong in the way he gained his wealth. He has not profited from dishonest gain. Neither is there any suggestion that the rich man is the cause of Lazarus's poverty. It is not that he is an employer paying exploitative wages or a relative failing to perform familial duties. As we saw earlier, close relationships would bring with them a level of obligation and reciprocity that would require generosity on the part of the rich man. But such a relationship is not implied here.

It could be argued that the rich man is no more responsible for Lazarus than you or I might be for anyone who happens to come knocking on our door either with personal needs or with a collecting box on behalf of someone else. We might even note that the rich man does not seek to drive Lazarus from his doorstep in the way many cities seek to "cleanse" their streets of beggars and street children. We need therefore to understand why he should be eternally banished to a place of torment while Lazarus appears to get first-class treatment and a fast-track ticket to the heavenly equivalent of a VIP lounge.

Our questioning must focus on the essential message of the parable. Kenneth Bailey (2008) notes that it contains many similarities to "Pearly Gate" stories that he has heard throughout the Middle East. They focus, often with humor, on someone trying to gain entrance to heaven after death. The stories, however, are not so much about the nature of life after death. Rather, they form a social comment on current social and political problems (p. 19). His comments remind us to keep in mind the social context of Jesus's day, where patrons and clients, a super-rich center and a poor and indebted periphery, defined the social structures.

However, it would be a mistake to read the parable as a simple case of the reversal of roles, or as a moral tale about riches and poverty. The parable has to be seen in the light of its ending with its reference to someone rising from the dead. The Pharisees, as we saw in in Luke 14, have behaved towards the poor, the crippled, the blind, and the lame in much the same way the rich man has to Lazarus. In doing so, they have ignored the testimony of the law and the prophets. If they will not listen to that witness, neither will they hear the voice of the one who will come back from the dead.

In Jesus we see God's future Kingdom breaking into the present. In his welcome of the poor and the outcast in this present life, he anticipates the Kingdom that is to come. But those who reject the poor, the Pharisees and all who ignore Lazarus at the gate, are rejecting more than this one beggar. So much more is at stake, for they are rejecting the Kingdom that Christ brings. It is to them that the parable stands as a timely, gracious, but uncomfortable warning.

A Parable of Gaps: The Literary Structure of the Rich Man and Lazarus

As we explore the passage in detail, it is important to look at the way Luke has structured it. The literary structure of the parable seems to mirror the story. It is a parable about a great chasm, and this is borne out in Luke's telling of it. We have two stories running side by side, stories of two people whose lives, as we will see later, never intersect.

The literary structure of this parable is developed around a stark contrast between the lives of the two characters. The parable is divided in two halves with the first half consisting of a story and the second half being built around a dialogue between Abraham and the rich man. In the table below, we see the way statements about one are paralleled with statements about the other in the first eight verses of the parable.

The Rich Man	THE GREAT CHASM	Lazarus
There was a rich man who was dressed in purple and fine linen		At his gate was laid a beggar named Lazarus, covered with sores
and lived in luxury every day.		and longing to eat what fell from the table. Even the dogs came and licked his sores.
The rich man also died and was buried.		And the time came when the beggar died and the angels carried him to Abraham's side.
In hell where he was in torment he looked up		And saw Abraham far away with Lazarus at his side.
So he called to him and said father Abraham have pity on me and send Lazarus to dip the tip of his finger in water and cool my tongue because I am in agony in this fire.		But Abraham replied, Son, remember in your lifetime you received your good things while Lazarus received bad things but now he is comforted in here and you are in agony. And besides all this a great chasm has been fixed so that those who want to go from here to you cannot, nor can anyone cross over there to us.

In the very structure of the parable, Luke identifies this key theme of the chasm. It defines the relationship between the principal characters. It is a chasm, created by the rich man for his own comfort in this life, which defines his relationship (or lack of it) with Lazarus and ultimately appears to define his relationship with God. It is a chasm built of blindness and indifference that lies at the heart of their nonrelationship. Bob Bell (2012) notes, "What is the chasm between the rich man and Lazarus? It is a chasm that still exists in the heart and mind of the rich man. He is unable to see or recognize the changed world he is in" (p. 75). The barrier of total indifference that he has constructed between himself and Lazarus in this life has, in death, been translated into to an impassable barrier that turns out not only to separate him from Lazarus but also from the faith of his ancestors. In separating himself from the poor, he has eternally separated himself from the blessings of God the Father.

The parable not only provides contrasts between their fates in this life and their fates in the afterlife but also highlights the eschatological reversal that has taken place. Their roles and conditions in this life are reversed in the next. So, in this life Lazarus longs for crumbs from the rich man's table (Luke 16:21); in the next life it is the rich man who longs for a drop of water from the tip of Lazarus's finger. Both seek something minimal from the other to ease their present suffering. Similarly, in the early life, Lazarus dwells in a hell of human misery, lying at the rich man's gate observing his banquet (Luke 16:21). In the afterlife, it is now the rich man who suffers in Hades, looking on to the heavenly banquet where Lazarus dines with Abraham (Luke 16:23). In the elemental needs of food, drink, and shelter, their roles have been eternally reversed, a reality the reader can observe but that the rich man needs to have spelled out to him (Luke 16:25).

Mapping the Gaps

As we look at the literary structure of the parable, we can see that the chasm that forms between the rich man and Lazarus is experienced at a number of levels. We see gaps that are spatial, economic, and relational. They reflect the different places the characters occupy in the story, the contrasts of wealth and poverty, and the lack of communication between them that runs through the whole parable.

Spatially, we can observe contrasts in the present life between "at the table" and "at the gate," and in the life to come where the chasm separates one who is in Hades from the one at the bosom of Abraham. The initial spatial difference had been small, from gate to table. Now it has become vast and impassable. Luke tells us the rich man, who has looked down at Lazarus from his table, must now look up in order to see Abraham and Lazarus who are now "far away."

The second dimension of the division is economic. The parable starkly contrasts the wealth of the rich man, with his fine food and fine clothes, with the poverty of the one who is covered in rags and sores. The economic gap between them is expressed in the most extreme terms. What is presented to us is the widest economic divide that Jesus's hearers could have conceived.

Third, and most profound, the gap is relational. One of the extraordinary aspects of this parable is that the two characters never speak to each other. Lazarus never speaks to anyone. In his poverty, he is totally passive. Action is done to him, first the depositing of him at the rich man's gate and later being carried by angels to the bosom of Abraham. He illustrates what it might mean for one's life to be robbed of all power and agency. He does not speak to the rich man, but critically, the rich man never speaks to him. Even in the afterlife communication is addressed via Abraham as an intermediary. There is no relationship between them even though the rich man appears to know his name.

It is these three gaps, spatial, economic, and relational, that provide some insight into the realities of an urbanizing world. We live in a world where advances in technology and communication alter our sense of space and physical distance. At one level, we are no longer as far apart as we once were; our world is shrinking. Yet economically, the centers of our world appear to be drifting further and further away from the peripheries. The gaps are widening both within nations and between them. We have the capacity to communicate across the globe, but not always across the street.

It is in the city that these divisions become most apparent. In cities, and in the gaps within and between them, we must constantly rekindle our imaginations as to what it means to share a common place, a common table and confront that which contributes to division and exclusion in urban space. We will need to find ways, in the name of Christ, to enter the gaps to reconfigure them, anticipating the day when the rich man and Lazarus share bread at one table.

Chapter 7
The Two-Story House

Jesus never speaks of wealth in itself or poverty in itself, but of rich and poor as they are, historically.

--Jose Miguez-Bonino

The Rich Man's Story

Words, if Lewis Carroll's Humpty Dumpty is to be believed, can mean anything we want them to mean. Perhaps he has a point. Words convey meaning, but the same word may conjure up very different images or ideas. So when Jesus says, "There was a rich man," what do we hear? We have seen that for Jesus's day, "rich" meant blessed by God. Wealth was often seen as a sign of divine pleasure. So to say there was a rich man wasn't such a distance in people's thinking from, "There was a good and righteous man." There was a rich man signified someone the hearers might aspire to be like.

As we read the text, we too will read through the lenses of our own culture. In Kenya it was once common to talk of the *Wabenzi*, those who drove a Mercedes-Benz. Rich means something different according to what our cultural and economic context is. I have met a man in a slum, living in a house without electricity or running water, who was described as rich because he owned and rented a number of similar properties. For some, rich means to have innumerable cows or goats; for others it is being a Bill Gates or a Donald Trump. For some, it is having a house with a pool; for others it is having a house with a tap. What we are to understand from the passage is that the man was rich in what might be thought of as an absolute sense rather than as purely a comparative measure. He was rich with a capital "R."

However one defines rich, it is what most of the world desires. In bookshops anywhere in the world, I am always struck by the number of self-help books that claim to offer routes to wealth and success. But when we read in Luke's Gospel, "There was a rich man," a set of warning bells should begin to go off. We have seen that the rich man of Luke 12 ends up as the dead fool with the big barn. The rich man of Luke 16:1–8 ends up cheated by his steward. So when in Luke 16:19 Jesus says, "There was a rich man," we should smell trouble.

As we have seen, the rich man of the parable is not just rich—he is super rich. He is not comfortable, he is not affluent, he is just unspeakably rich. More than that, his wealth is out there for all to see. He is not quietly rich, discreetly rich; he is ostentatiously rich. Jesus spells this out using things that symbolized the wealth of his day—his attire, food, and house. First, we are told he dressed in purple robes and fine linen. Purple was the most expensive clothing, reserved for the finest of occasions. It was expensive because the dye to make it was only obtainable from the murex shellfish (Morris, 1974, p. 252). This is the color used in the 10 curtains of the tabernacle (Ex. 26:1) and of Aaron's sacred garments. It is the ceremonial color of high priests and kings, but the everyday wear of this rich man. Hidden beneath his purple robes, he wears fine linen—nothing but the best!

From his clothing, we move swiftly to his table. Luke records that this man lived in luxury every day. We are told that he feasted every day. The verb used here, *euphrainomenos* is the same word used to describe the feast put on by the father on the return of the lost son in Luke 15:23 (Morris, 1974, p. 252). The occasion of celebration to mark the homecoming of the lost son is the daily fare of the rich man. What the world would call a banquet, he merely calls lunch. Bailey (2008) notes that if he feasted like this every day, then Jesus's hearers would know he wasn't keeping the Sabbath and would not have been giving his servants a day of rest. It seems that this rich man, by his lifestyle, violates the Ten Commandments week (p. 22).

Finally, we have the man's dwelling as an example of his wealth. Luke tells us nothing about the man's home but there is a clue in the reference to the gate. According to Darrell Bock (1996), the word used here suggests the gate of a significant property or estate. It is a word often associated with entrances to cities, temples, and palaces (p. 1366). Stephen Wright (2000) notes that this is not a simple gate but more likely an ornamental entrance way (p. 230). It is at this entrance that Lazarus sits.

Lazarus's Story

We are presented, therefore, with a violent contrast between the rich man and Lazarus. In describing Lazarus's situation, Jesus presents us not with one who is poor, but with one who is absolutely poor, who possesses nothing, who lives in abject and degraded poverty, robbed of all human dignity. He is positioned at the rich man's gate. Their lives are close to each other spatially but a world apart in every other respect. We read that he is laid at the rich man's gate. This would suggest he is crippled in some way and incapable of getting there without the assistance of others (Schweizer, 1984). Joel Green (1997) notes that the verb translated "laid at the gate," *ebebgeto*, could equally refer to being thrown down, making Lazarus look like litter on the rich man's doorstep (p. 606).

Kenneth Bailey (2008) suggests that when we are told Lazarus is laid at the rich man's gate, what is implied is that the community knows the rich man alone has the resources to help Lazarus and so faithfully, every day, they carry him to the rich man's gate (p.22). It is as if the community is doing what they can with the resources available to them only for Lazarus to be studiously ignored by the one who is most able to assist him. As we have seen elsewhere in Luke, it is not to the rich that the poor should look for help. In the patron-client relationship this rich man would look to the village for honor and status in the community, but he will offer nothing in return.

To add to Lazarus's misery, we are told he was covered in sores. Here is a figure reminiscent of Job but lacking even a shard of pottery to scrape his sores (Job 2:8). Instead, he is facing the indignity of being licked by dogs. There is bitter irony here. Even the wild dogs, in licking his sores, offer him more comfort than the rich man.

In this position of poverty, despair, and hunger, he looks at the rich man's table. Like the lost son of the previous chapter who longs to feed on the food given to pigs, Lazarus in turn longs for scraps falling from the table, which no doubt at least the dogs will get to eat. Some commentators suggest Lazarus longed for the loaves of bread that were used like napkins and discarded next to the table. Either way, here is a man with nothing at the gate of a man with everything, and he dies with nothing.

The inequality of their lives is mirrored in their deaths. Lazarus dies, and we are simply told that the angels carried him to Abraham's side. There is no mention of a burial. As with many societies, appropriate burial was essential to the Jews of Jesus's day. To be refused burial, to be left to the dogs and carrion like refuse in the street was tantamount to being cursed by God (Green, 1997, p. 607). Yet that appears to be the fate of Lazarus. The rich man, we are simply told, was buried.

From the moment of death, the eschatological reversal is spelled out in the boldest of colors. Lazarus, the poor, unclean beggar, finds himself in the arms of Abraham. He occupies the highest place in the assembly of the righteous and has discovered God is in fact the God of the poor and the destitute (Jeremias, 1972, p. 184). The rich man, on the other hand, the one so apparently blessed by God, is now experiencing great torment in Hades.

Trading Places

How the roles have changed! Once it was Lazarus looking longingly through the gates to a rich man who appears not to even recognize his existence. Now it is the rich man looking longingly in the direction of Lazarus who is seated at Abraham's side. Apparently still unaware of the depth and permanency of his predicament, he calls out across the chasm that divides them.

"Father Abraham." These are telling words. He addresses Abraham as a child of the faith who knows Abraham to be his father. Yet his understanding of what it means to be a child of Abraham is deeply flawed. In Luke 3:8, John the Baptist reminds the crowds that if God so wishes he can produce sons of Abraham out of a pile of rocks. It soon becomes clear that the rich man might as well be a pile of rocks for all the good his presumed relationship with Abraham will do him. For true children of Abraham, membership among God's people is not an inherited status. Rather, they are those who have listened to Moses and the Prophets and have displayed the goodness and open-handed generosity and mercy of God, particularly to those in need (Green, 1997, p. 23). This is something the rich man appears to know very little about. His request indicates he is yet to understand the reversal of his and Lazarus's fortunes. He may have been very rich, but he appears not to have been very bright.

His words that follow are deeply ironic: "Have pity on me." He appeals for mercy to Abraham, seemingly oblivious to his own failure to help the one whose only help was from God ("Lazarus" means "he whom God helps"). The rich man is aware of Lazarus's name; he has ignored him, but he is not unaware of his existence. However, his request is not addressed to Lazarus. Even in his dire condition, he will not lower himself to speak to Lazarus, but instead directs his request to Abraham to "send Lazarus" as if he might at least act as his personal servant.

The rich man's appeal is to the generous hospitality of Abraham, the one who had unknowingly entertained angels (Gen. 18:1–15). Yet the request comes from one who has failed to show the most elementary hospitality to the one, helped by God alone, who now sits at Abraham's side. During his life on earth, he gave not one crumb; in the next life, he receives not one drop. Just in case it has slipped the rich man's notice, he is reminded in no uncertain terms that the roles have changed (Luke 16:25). Not only have they changed positions, but more worrying for the rich man who is slowly getting the message, their positions have also become fixed. The great chasm that he created on his own doorstep, which so shielded his life from the pain and unpleasantness of Lazarus's existence, has now become a permanent and unbridgeable gap that neither can cross. He has, so to speak, dug his own grave.

Too Little Too Late

At this point, we finally see the rich man exercise some concern for others. Yet the concern is for his own, his brothers, who one suspects are well on the road to the same fate. Lazarus the lackey is the first choice for the rich man who still has not grasped the change in their relative status. Interesting, the man who could never get past his own gate is now being invited (albeit indirectly through Abraham) to do some door-to-door visits to his brothers. One has to assume at this point that the rich man has observed a radical change in Lazarus's appearance or he would be unlikely to make it past the gate, let alone into conversation with the brothers. But Abraham will have none of it. They have Moses and the Prophets, he says to the rich man. And of course, here is the rub. The rich man has not been the victim of a tricky change in the rules. The law and the Prophets have spelled it out from the beginning: love your neighbor, love justice and show mercy, exercise concern for the poor, the stranger, the hungry. This is not some radical new teaching that required a special envoy to explain. It is there for his brothers to see just as it was for him.

At this point, the man who has never lacked anything, who has always, one suspects, got the things he has demanded, resorts to special pleading. But if someone goes back from the dead they will repent, he says. The word "repent" suggests the man with the money has finally got the message. A change of heart, life, behavior, and attitude is what will save them and perhaps something as dramatic as a man back from the dead would be convincing, he reasons. The man back from the dead he most likely has in mind is Lazarus, errand boy extraordinaire, whom Abraham still seems unwilling to send. Abraham does not point out that since Lazarus went so completely unnoticed in his past life, a trip back from the dead might still not register with his presumably similarly myopic brothers.

Abraham's response is telling: They already have everything they need to know in order to do as God requires of them. A visitor from the dead will not change that. But the words at the close of the parable spill out beyond the rich man and his pampered brothers. Luke leaves them hanging like a question mark over the heads of the readers. Is it possible to have encountered the one risen from the dead and still fail to be convinced of what Moses and the Prophets require in our encounters with the Lazaruses of this life?

When the emphasis falls on the end of the parable, we see this parable is not ultimately a comment on social problems. Certainly it offers characters who are types, representing the poles of an unequal society, a society under judgment (N.T. Wright, 2004, p. 231). However, the purpose of the parable is not simply a social critique. The second half of the parable is set in Hades, which is a place in Jewish tradition that was the destiny of all people, sometimes with the expected outcome of a later judgment already mapped out through the separation of the wicked and the righteous (Green, 1997, p. 607). The parable simply makes use of that tradition to communicate truth. That truth is not that the poor should console themselves with the hope of recompense beyond the grave (Adeyemo, 2006, p. 1237). We have already seen that Luke presents Jesus as one in whom eschatological reversal already takes place. "Blessed are you who hunger now" (Luke 6:21). The message of Good News to the poor is a present reality, not just a future hope. Ultimately this parable is not about Lazarus at all; it is about the rich man and the brothers. It could even be retitled the parable for the six brothers, for it comes as a warning, like Noah to the flood generation, of the eternal consequences of self-centered living and ignoring the needs of the poor (Jeremias, 1972, p. 186).

The rich man, in African terms, has failed to practice ubuntu. He has not acknowledged Lazarus as a fellow human being. In a life characterized by individualism, by a refusal to share his bread with the poor, he has become detestable in God's sight (Adeyemo, 2006, 1237). Like the priest and the Levite of Luke 10, in the pursuit of a life of ease, uncomplicated by the plight of others, he has failed to see his neighbor and in so doing failed to comprehend what it is to be a true child of Abraham, a true son of the covenant. For at the heart of this chapter is the message that faithfulness to God is demonstrated in hospitality to the poor.

Locating Ourselves in the Parable

Jesus's parables often seem to invite the hearer to consider with whom they identify in the story. Are we like the Pharisee or the tax collector in Luke 18? Which of the characters are we on the dangerous road from Jerusalem to Jericho, or how do we locate ourselves in the parable of the lost son? However, the extreme positions of the rich man and Lazarus perhaps make it difficult to identify ourselves with either of the main characters. It is unlikely that we are so unspeakably rich and so callously ambivalent to the poor that we feel an affinity with the rich man. Yet neither are we Lazarus, whose absolute poverty renders him utterly passive, with no voice or action of his own. Of course the parable does not offer a blunt choice. Both characters represent something far from God's purpose and intention for humanity. But we are still left with the difficult question of how it speaks to us in the realities of our own context.

The rich man and Lazarus are not the only characters in the parable. There is Abraham as well. In one Bible study where I asked people to locate themselves in the story, one person described a strong sense of affinity with Abraham. I was slightly taken aback by this suggestion until he began to explain how he often found himself pressed into the position of mediator between economically and racially divided communities with people attempting to communicate through him rather than directly with each other. In particular, people from more affluent churches and communities would speak to him rather than making the conscious effort to cross boundaries and speak directly with those at the margins of the city. This was, for him, an often uncomfortable and entirely unsought role. For those who similarly find themselves pushed or drawn into such a role, the parable seems only to highlight the contours of noncommunication rather than giving hope of overcoming them. The rich man's conversation with Abraham will not end up being a redemptive one. That is part of the deep irony of the parable. Access to father Abraham will never serve to offset the rich man's failure to address the man at the gate. The gap is spoken across but never breached. Even Abraham cannot overcome the eternal gulf the rich man has unknowingly constructed.

It is easy and perhaps occasionally attractive to find ourselves in Abraham's position, mediating between communities that never meet or speak. It is undeniably a place some will actively seek, while others are rightly nervous of it. For it is potentially a place of power that can be used to consolidate the position of the mediator while doing little to challenge or even mitigate the roots of division. In this sense, it is a role that is deeply flawed. Abraham can console and comfort Lazarus, but he can offer little comfort or hope to the rich man. Redemption would have required a transformation of the gap that would bring the rich man and Lazarus face to face in the same space. Abraham could speak across the gap that divides them, but it would have taken both the rich man and Lazarus together to transform the divide.

Abraham may appear as a mediator, but his words illustrate the limitations of his role. He is not a mediator in the true sense of the word. He does not hold a neutral position between two camps. He is firmly and eternally with Lazarus. He is at his side and on his side, and so is powerless to help the rich man or his family for which he belatedly makes appeal.

There is always a place for mediation in seeking to bring healing and reconciliation between communities that have long since lost the will or even the language to communicate directly with each other. Cities can become so divided that it becomes difficult to find the spaces, words, and gestures that make redemptive conversations possible. It is perhaps in those places that our vocation is not to be Abraham but rather Lazarus in the midst of those who otherwise might not see him.

My friend Richard, a pastor from Kibera, was invited on short notice to address a group of senior public figures in a five-star hotel in Nairobi. The highly prominent individual who was billed for the event could not attend and Richard, ever an entertaining speaker, was his last-minute stand-in. Relishing the moment, Richard introduced himself to his immaculately dressed audience and announced that he was from Kibera. There was a palpable shock around the room and perhaps a sense that they had been fooled in some way to find themselves being addressed by a man from Kibera. By the end of the morning, their impressions had changed and they had been won over, convinced, challenged, and entertained. But the power of his words came not because he spoke about a place, as I might have done, but because he spoke from it. It was as if Lazarus had entered the room and spoken.

While our lives may be far removed from the world experienced by Lazarus, one senses we are still invited to find some kind of solidarity with him. We are invited into a closer identification with Lazarus in the very way Jesus identified himself with the poor and the outcast. But what form might that take?

A funeral rite of the Roman Catholic Church includes these words of committal:

May choirs of angels welcome you
and lead you to the bosom of Abraham;

and where Lazarus is poor no longer
may you find eternal rest.

In the expectation of eternity, the prayer invites us to identify ourselves with Lazarus. His future life is one that is seen to embody our own hopes and expectations. We are encouraged by the hope of an eternity in a place of abundant blessing, provision, and security. We hope we will find ourselves seated with Lazarus at Abraham's side. But this poses a difficult question: How can we seek to identify with Lazarus in the coming age if we do not identify with him in this one? For surely we cannot create two Lazaruses—one in whose destiny we hope to share and one who still lingers at our gate.

Chapter 8

The Divided City

Much violence is based on the illusion that life is a property to be defended and not a gift to be shared.

--Henri Nouwen

Kawangware and Lavington: Where Far Can Be Near and Near Can Be Out of Sight

Kawangware is a community of informal and permanent housing on the western fringes of Nairobi and a place where we at the Centre for Urban Mission have worked over the years. It is also a place that, in a very particular way, illustrates the realities of the divided city.

One approach to Kawangware is through the leafy suburb of Lavington. Situated at a higher elevation than much of Nairobi, amid broad avenues of Jacaranda trees, are the bungalows, town houses, and serviced apartments of one of Nairobi's elite communities. Traveling along one of its avenues, where access is regulated by security barriers, you eventually come to a road between two large dwellings. Journeying up this lane, the landscape changes rapidly. Large residential homes suddenly give way to smaller iron-sheet businesses and dwellings and single-room residential blocks with the upper-level incomplete, awaiting funds to build another storey.

Somewhere along this road, it is good to stop and take in the scene. On one side is Kawangware, alive with people, noise, and activity. Bars blast music, delicious smells of frying food emanate from small stalls, and farther down are the more pungent smells of home brewing. All around is the constant movement of people of all ages. This is a vibrant community, trying to establish a firmer foothold in the city. It is a place of enterprise and innovation that is growing and developing but largely devoid of central planning and regulation. It illustrates what Andrew Hake (1997), decades earlier, described as the self-help city where urban services are generated by the innovation and creativity of local residents. Open sewers, a tangle of informal electricity connections, and the large number of water vendors reveal both the lack of government services and the capacity of a community to improvise. This is a community on the fringes of Nairobi, where people live both geographically and, in the majority of cases, economically at the margins of the city.

As you look out across Kawangware, to your left is a wall. In places it is about four meters high. Above the wall are spirals of razor wire and above the razor wire is an electric fence. On my last visit a further addition was in place. A screen of green netting had been erected, perhaps designed to give some visual relief to the occupants of newly constructed town houses whose homes are situated on the other side of the wall in Lavington.

This dividing wall provides a stark image of the divided city and has, over the years, been the site of many informal seminars conducted by the Centre for Urban Mission. In every case, we have been on the Kawangware side of the wall. The other side, Lavington, is most definitely private space.

The wall raises many questions. What is it that is so feared? What does the wall represent to both communities, and what does it say about the way we perceive and relate to one another? In what sense can we claim to be citizens of the same city while constructing such impenetrable barriers between us?

In Ephesians, Paul speaks of the dividing wall of hostility that has separated Jew and Gentile and that has been broken down in the person of Jesus Christ (Eph 2:14). Yet the Kawangware/Lavington wall remains intact. Even more starkly, in modern day Israel/Palestine new walls have been created that both feed on and produce the sense of hostility and threat they are supposed to remove. Around the world, protective barriers stand as symbols of communities separated by much more than the concrete and steel erected between them.

If I stand in Kawangware and look above the wall to the suburban homes beyond, I could be tempted to criticize those who live on the other side of the razor wire. Yet three things constrain me. The first is the sense that this wall is an impoverishment of both communities. I haven't met the owners of the houses, but I suspect they are in some ways imprisoned by the walls that surround them. They are not free to enjoy or experience their neighbors while they are separated from the perceived chaos or threat lying just beyond their boundaries. These barriers of anxiety prevent social contact, furthering isolation and diminishing community.

Second, I am aware of my personal involvement in the wall. If I follow the line of the wall, in the end it will come to a large international school with an equally high wall. It is the school our children attended. I have an investment in the wall—whether I choose it to be there or not. My own place in the city of Nairobi is, in some measure, bound up in the bricks and mortar that isolate one community from another. Sometimes we have to begin by confronting the way the threads of our own lives form part of the wider fabric of division and injustice. We need to be honest about the inconsistencies within our own lives and the conflicts between our idealized selves and the people we actually are in a given situation. But we cannot stop there. While it is generally beyond our powers to remove the embedded and concrete expressions of division in society, it should never be beyond us to find ways to openly engage with the worlds that these physical walls separate us from.

Chris Heuertz and Christine Pohl (2010), in their wonderful book *Friendship at the Margins*, address with great honesty the inconsistencies and conflicts that come from seeking to move beyond some of these complex barriers. It is an experience I am all too familiar with, and like many others, I struggle to find the necessary courage or conviction to navigate them well. At times, there seems to be wisdom in recognizing the limits to our capacity to cross such boundaries and to the depth of our identification with those on the other side of the wall. I have marched with slum dwellers in Nairobi in protest at the selling of the land beneath their feet to wealthy property speculators. But when, with great humor and determination, they formed a sit-in blocking the gates of the Land Ministry, as a foreign national I would only stand, in rather more careful and limited solidarity, at the pavement edge. Sometimes our calling is to stand at the margins, at the outer edge of places of conflict and division and pray. But so often the limits of my crossing of boundaries has not been a product of such godly discretion, but of an unwillingness to confront the cost, discomfort, or inconvenience of what might be involved. The issue here is not that as an outsider I have the means or capacity to make any significant difference to these situations—far from it. Rather, it is that the Gospel calls us into solidarity with those at the margins and into the challenging questions of how that is best lived out.

The third aspect of the wall between Kawangware and Lavington is that it has a history and represents more than either those who constructed it or those who live along it now alone could say. It did not emerge in some accidental or haphazard way. It was constructed along the border, created in the British colonial era, between the area of the city designated for European settlement (Lavington) and the area outside the boundary of the city, which was for African settlement (Kawangware). Its bricks and mortar symbolize more profound and enduring divisions.

Just as Paul reminds the Ephesian Church that the dividing wall of hostility has been overcome in Christ (Eph 2:14), so he also reminds them that their struggle is not with flesh and blood (or brick and mortar), but with "the powers of this dark world" (Eph 6:12). The root problem is something much deeper than the wall and the individuals located in this most visibly divided place. The fundamental problem lies within forces of evil, of the segregation and exclusion that the wall simply embodies. Those forces, too, have a history.

Spatial Division and the Postcolonial City

Nairobi was a colonial city. Until the period leading up to independence, the geography of the city was constructed around racial segregation with much of the right to the city the almost exclusive domain of the European. The colonial administration planned for European settlement and regarded Africans as purely temporary sojourners in the city, making little provision for their accommodation (Obudho, 1997, p. 317).

The mind-set of colonialism created the initial shape of Nairobi. It was a city constructed on the basis of spatial injustice. Throughout much of Africa, the primary basis of colonial town planning was the segregation of the "white man's city" from the "native villages" (Elate, 2004, p. 54). Segregation either followed natural barriers such as hills and rivers or through artificially constructed barriers creating buffer zones between communities.

Those structures of inequality, once racial, have in the independence era become economic. Father Alex Zanotelli, one of Nairobi's more radical Catholic priests, argued Nairobi had transitioned from ethnic to economic apartheid. While this is an overstatement that risks diluting our understanding of the full horror of the offense of apartheid, it is clear that structures of racial inequality, laid with the foundations of the city, continue to give physical and moral shape to modern Nairobi and other cities that share a similar history.

The development of cities arising from the legacy of the grossly distorted foundations of colonialism is not unique to Nairobi. The majority of capital cities in Africa were established in the colonial era.

Similarly, many cities in Asia and South America have grown and developed out of a legacy of colonialism. The challenge of postcolonial governments has been to reconfigure cities in ways that no longer exhibit the DNA of segregation and inequality of an earlier era. That has been hard to achieve. Achille Mbembe, in The Post Colony, raises the difficult question: "Have we really entered another period, or do we find the same theatre, the same mimetic acting, with different actors and spectators but with the same convulsions and the same insults? Can we really talk of moving beyond colonialism?" (Mbembe, as cited by G. Myers, 2011, p. 46).

Clearly there are many ways cities have moved beyond their colonial legacy. The sheer social, cultural, geographic, and economic vitality and diversity of postcolonial cities are evidence of that. However, the wall in Kawangware illustrates the way the legacy of colonialism can still shape structures of relationships in cities in the way Mbembe suggests. It has proved immensely difficult to subvert the inherited urban forms in ways that no longer reflect the imposed inequality and segregation of an earlier era, but rather embody some of the traditional cultures and values that they displaced (Elate, 2004, p. 51).

But is this spatial injustice purely a function of postcolonial cities? Were Western industrial cities built on far more benign foundations? Fredrick Engels observed that Manchester and other industrial capitalist cities tended to develop concentrically around a dominant center with radial wedges of wealth and poverty. Such cities produced and maintained geographies that gave greater advantage and higher status to the wealthy residents (Engels, as cited by Soja, 2010, p.48). While post-industrial cities are radically different to the places they once were, the social structures of privilege and marginalization, embodied with urban space, remain largely intact. The nature and extent of social division vary widely between cities and nations, yet almost every major world city today has growing polarities of the highly privileged and protected citadel and the poverty and isolation of the ghetto.

In the 1960s, Henri Lefebvre coined the phrase "the right to the city," arguing that those most negatively affected by urban life should have greater say in the direction and shaping of the city (Lefebvre, as quoted by Butler, 2014). Today cities still face the question of how well they represent the rights and interests of those who are at the political, social, and economic margins. Increasing degrees of social exclusion; communities resisting processes of gentrification in which longstanding residents find themselves displaced by rising land and property prices; and the redlining of communities that prevent them from being able to access loans and insurance, all illustrate the ways space in cities can become either contested or marginalized.

Against this background, Susan Fainstein (2010) presents the case for the just city, the city where public investment and regulation produce more equitable outcomes rather than supporting those already well off (p. 3). Our thinking about urban mission must take us into precisely these territories as we seek to reimagine cities in ways that illustrate and embody our understanding of God's justice. In the city, we need to ensure our mission thinking is informed by a sense of what the just city, or the good city, might look like.

Mind the Gap

Chapter 9
Where Money Doesn't Talk: The Economic and Relational Gap

The truth is, our civilization is not Christian; it is a tragic compound of great ideal and fearful practice, of loving charity and fearful clutching of possessions.

--Alan Paton, *Cry, The Beloved Country*

Coca-Cola in Korogocho

Jack is a night watchman. He moved into Korogocho informal settlement a few years ago. He is from the Maasai community. Generations of guarding goats and herds against lions and other predators has given his community the skills and courage that make them effective and sought-after guards. Many have moved to Nairobi for work because their pastoral lifestyle is increasingly threatened as land is sold for real estate and farming. In spite of their skills, the salary of a security guard can be pitifully small.

Jack came to faith in Nairobi and is now part of a small Anglican church that meets in an iron-sheet building in Korogocho. One Sunday I went with two of the church evangelists to visit him and his family. We were greeted warmly and invited inside a small hut divided by a simple curtain. Behind the curtain, a child on a bed was coughing, clearly unwell. We each sat on one of the three chairs in the room, and then Jack asked us to wait. He rushed out. Meanwhile Jack's wife explained that one of the children was very sick. The edge of the curtain was drawn back to reveal a small child who was clearly struggling to breathe. The small hut with little ventilation did not seem to be helping matters. The parents had taken her to a doctor but medical help was expensive.

Moments later Jack returned with a broad smile and armfuls of Coca-Cola. He had bought each of us one of the larger bottles. My heart sank. I thought about the child behind the curtain and the cost of the Coca-Cola, which I knew I did not need. We prayed, giving thanks, and then the bottles were opened, and I drank.

Sitting in the room, I began to calculate the cost of the bottles of Coke to Jack. Between us we have drunk half of their daily household income. I then began to calculate what half of my daily income would be. Would I joyfully offer it in hospitality to a stranger, with or without the added challenge of attending a sick child?

My description of the visit to Jack's home would be repeated in different ways many times during my time in Nairobi. It is a story thousands of others might equally tell with a similar confusion of feeling. Of course it raises all the issues of what happens when those who are resource-rich are entertained by those who are resource-poor. But where does the problem lie in the story? I am troubled, but by what? There are whole histories of injustice in the story. There's the way rural poverty frequently forces families to migrate to cites, often to live at levels barely above subsistence; the way companies pay salaries that cannot constitute a living wage; and the way this hard-earned money was going to contribute to the seemingly endless profits of a massive multinational corporation. I could have been concerned about those things, but I suspect they were not at the forefront of my mind. I was troubled because through my eyes Jack was poor and I was not, but he was showing a generosity towards me that I doubt I would have shown to him in different circumstances.

When author Alan Paton writes of "loving charity and a fearful clutching of possessions," I fear I understand only too well the sentiments he describes. But this is my perception of the situation. It is not Jack's. I may consider him poor, but he defies that description as he enters the room with an armful of bottles. He is a man who can be generous and hospitable with what he has. If I have a problem with that, then that is my problem. I have found myself as the receiver in a relationship with someone who, economically, has much less than I have. My sense is that this should have been the other way around, but in Jack's home he defines the relationship, and in it he is the host and I am the guest.

Rich and Poor in the Global City

On September 21, 2013 a group of armed men and women entered Nairobi's Westgate shopping mall and began shooting indiscriminately at shoppers and staff. It marked the start of a terrible three days of terror that took the lives of more than 60 people. The events were international news in the way other tragedies in an African city would not have been. Two years earlier, about 100 people died when petrol from an oil pipeline leaked into the storm water drains and exploded in the middle of a small but densely populated informal settlement called Sinai, in Nairobi's industrial area. It was widely reported at the time but captured the attention of the international media for only a brief period. Assurances were given about rehousing those affected, but in the end the story faded along with many of the promises to those who had been made homeless.

These two places, Westgate and Sinai, reflect the extremes of a city like Nairobi. The tragedy at Westgate caught the attention of the media, partly because it was an appalling story that kept unfolding, but also because it was a genuinely global event. Westgate was a sign and symbol of Nairobi as a truly global city. This upscale mall, with marble floors, cinema complexes, and outlets for global brands could have been anywhere in the world. It caters to affluent Kenyans and appeals to the tastes of an international community that Nairobi has so successfully attracted over the years. The names and faces of those who died or were injured demonstrated, in a most tragic way, the truly international nature of this mall. The same could not be said of Sinai.

Nairobi is a globalizing city. But like many cities around the world that compete to become hubs of influence in the network of the global economy, it pays a high price, in terms of equitability, for a place at the table.

One of the paradoxes of globalization is that while the world is said to be getting smaller, in economic terms we are getting ever further apart. Castells (2000) notes how in the last 30 years of the 20th century the divide between the world's rich and poor expanded massively with increased inequality and polarization in the distribution of wealth. He noted that over this period the share of income of the richest 20% of the world's population had increased from 74% to 85%, while the share of the poorest 20% had fallen from 2.3% to 1.4 % with a third of the world's population living at or below subsistence level (pp. 78–81). Current trends, as Castells predicted, suggest a further widening of that gap. This trend between nations also was mirrored within them as levels of intracountry inequality increased in most parts of the world. The Gini coefficient, which measures levels of inequality, grew in the majority of countries, with the United Kingdom having the fastest increase in inequality among all the countries in the Organisation for Economic Co-operation and Development. If the French economist Thomas Piketty (2014) is correct, and if current trends are not arrested, then the 21st century will see an ever-growing increase in financial inequality and ever-growing poverty.

Somewhere within the constant clamor for economic growth, technological development, and the burning desire to acquire and accumulate, we have to ask fundamental questions about the kind of world we want to live in and what that means for all humanity in present and future generations.

The Logic of Globalization

The vast gap between how events at Westgate and Sinai were covered in the press is an aspect of the logic of the global city. If cities in the developing world want to attract foreign capital and investment, they must develop the kind of infrastructure and lifestyle opportunities that come with it. For this reason, it often appears to make more sense to invest in high-speed internet technology in one part of the city rather than safe drinking water in another. The demands of the global economy mean investment in infrastructure development is often directed to the most privileged areas of cities in order to, in some sense, keep in the race. Saskia Sassen (1999) notes the way globalization produces an "over valorization" of certain parts of the city and its economy in comparison to others. By this she means certain places, occupations, and forms of economic activity become far more highly valued than others, creating ever-widening gaps between people and places.

One example of this gap can be observed in access to water. In Nairobi, it is estimated that those living in the informal settlement areas of the city pay as much as eight times more for their water than those living in the formal area. Members of our congregation at St. Jerome in Kibera would be up hours before daylight to collect water in plastic containers from private water vendors. By eight in the morning, if they were to get their water, they would have to join the long queues snaking their way around Kibera's tracks. Within the water charge is a fee for sanitation services, but for the vast majority of the community, sanitation is a pit latrine dug and emptied by the community. In contrast, those, like myself, living in the formal area of the city pay the Nairobi Water Company a fraction of what was paid by the residents of Kibera and in return had the benefit of sanitation through a public sewage system.

Informal Settlements and the Relational Divide

In 2007, the Centre for Urban Mission held the first of what became a series of biannual conferences aimed at bringing together churches and Christian organizations from around the city of Nairobi to take a fresh and more coordinated look at mission in the city. Our first conference was entitled "Re-Imagining the City." Its aim was ambitious. Mindful that we lived in such a divided city, we sought to imagine Nairobi differently. Very consciously influenced by Walter Brueggemann's (2001) book *The Prophetic Imagination*, we sought to kick-start a process whereby people from different parts of a socially and economically divided city could imagine together a different kind of future. We all recognized the need for change, but the critical question was whether there was any shared vision for what that change might look like.

The conference represented a significant step forward in terms of heightening awareness of the challenges the churches faced in the city, but there were aspects of the event that we undoubtedly got wrong. In a desire to attract sufficient interest in the event, we invited a number of high-profile speakers from large churches and movements in the city. However, there was a subterranean disquiet among some of the delegates who felt their voices were not being adequately heard. The situation came to a head after an excellent presentation by a leader of one of the most dynamic and affluent churches in the city. In time set aside for dialogue with the speaker, a pastor working in Kibera, challenged the speaker to come and visit his community, walk in his shoes, and see the city from a different perspective. There then followed a brief exchange that created the sort of buzz within the room that indicated we were finally discussing the real issues.

This very public conversation highlighted the deep division existing within the city that was reflected in churches as much as anywhere else. It became apparent that both pastors, from two very different parts of Nairobi, felt that neither had access to the other's area of ministry or to one another. They had become chaplains to a fragmented city, and all the social barriers and distances that exist between slums and private estates seemed to be mirrored in their relationship in the room. It took one person to have the courage and perception to expose the reality of the situation, and the other to have the grace to listen and respond, in order to move the conversation forward.

We have seen that one of the most disturbing aspects of the parable of the rich man and Lazarus is the total absence of any form of communication between the two. Lazarus never speaks, and the rich man only addresses Lazarus through Abraham. There seems no possibility of either reaching out to the other and entering the space that has grown between them. It is this silence, this non-relationship, which makes it impossible to address the other gaps that divide them.

The conversation at the conference in 2007 was undeniably the most talked-about aspect of the whole event and helped us begin to rethink what the next steps might be. Someone had to take the initiative, breaking the silence and speaking into the void. In later conferences, pastors would speak of crossing the tracks and entering into each other's worlds and bridging gaps between the communities. There is still a massive distance to travel on that agenda, but on that morning in 2007 we at least caught a glimpse of the journey that lay ahead and the possibility of navigating it.

Broken and fractured relationships, Bryant Myers (1999) reminds us, lie at the very heart of situations of poverty. Poverty, he says, emerges from a whole cluster of broken relationships that include our relationships with one another, with creation, with God and with ourselves. He argues that any attempts to deal with poverty must begin by addressing the broken and corrupted relationships that create and maintain the very structures that keep the poor poor.

Changing Perspective

Not long after joining St. Jerome Parish in Kibera, I had a conversation with Janet, a member of the choir. It was a conversation that forced me to reconsider the way I understood the community where I worshiped. Janet was a leading member of the choir and a longstanding member of the congregation. In the course of our conversation she indicated she worked in the administration of a large public university. I was a bit surprised, since she lived in Kibera. I pointed out that she must have a long commute most mornings. She laughed. She had a flat at the university and came to Kibera on the weekends. It slowly dawned on me that here was someone who did not have to live in Kibera. She had other, undoubtedly better, accommodations elsewhere in Nairobi. Why are you here, I found myself asking. It was a decision that at the time made no sense to me. She simply looked around the church and told me that this is where her family is, where here friends are, and this is where she likes to be when she is not at work.

It is easy to make dangerous generalizations about any community and to make outside judgments that are disturbingly ignorant of internal realities. Any community is far more than the physical environment it occupies. There is much written about slums and informal settlements that point to them as places of appalling poverty, squalor, and deprivation—as problems needing a solution. Statistics on basic issues of household income, access to water and electricity, rates of morbidity, and infant mortality all tell a common story, but it is only part of the story. So much literature of slums, and perhaps most of the literature generated by the NGOs that work in them, define slums in terms of deficit and dysfunction. They are places defined by a countless array of needs. Yet, as Janet gently informed me, they are also places of community and belonging with rich resources of their own. I have since discovered they are places of innovation and creativity and with a much wider range of people than the stereotypes might lead us to believe. They are home to students and graduates, medical professionals and teachers, entrepreneurs and craftsman, as well as the chronically low paid and unemployed. When Jesus told us not to be deceived into making judgments by appearance but discern what lies beneath those first impressions, he could well have been talking about Kibera.

Slums are unquestionably symbols and manifestations of urban inequality. They are the unjust city written large on the urban landscape. They reflect the way land, resources, and the good of the city are unevenly and inequitably distributed. In Nairobi, it is estimated that 60% of the population live on just 5% of the residential land. They are often the hangover of colonial policies, which systematically ignored the needs of indigenous populations, and the policies of the postcolonial governments that preceded them. They cannot be understood apart from the processes of globalization or the neoliberal policies that have been imposed upon so much of the developing world (Parsons, 2010). Yet they also reflect the aspirations and hopes of millions who want to find opportunity in the global marketplace, which is located in the city.

This tension between slums as symbols of urban failure, inequity, and spatial injustice, and slums as places of opportunity, entrepreneurship, and urbanization from below is evident in much of the literature. Doug Saunders (2011) provides a convincing argument that slums do not simply contain marginal people, a victimized underclass, but rather are frequently places that house the central actors in many urban economies, effectively renewing and expanding the city while temporarily located at the sidelines. He notes the way urbanization has provided the fastest route out of rural poverty. That route, for many, is marked by transition through *favelas*, bustees, slums, or informal settlements into a more secure and permanent life in the city.

While Saunders' statements may be overoptimistic, he does provide a helpful counterbalance to those who see slums in purely negative terms. In a similar vein, writers such as AbdouMaliq Simone (2004) point to the dynamism of slums and informal settlements and the ways their informality creates new and viable forms of urbanization, in contrast to more Western forms of urban expansion. Simone argues against the notion that the formal economy is that which is real and normative, posing the question of whether the informal sector could act as a platform for a different kind of sustainable urban configuration (p. 70).

Yet amid the arguments around the growth of informal settlements, there remains the reality that slums and informal settlements often provide a concrete and spatial expression of deeper social divisions and social exclusion. For all the diversity to be found among those living in informal settlements, there remains the reality that these are communities that are often separated, physically and economically, from the more formal areas of cities, and these separations are also experienced relationally. The spatial and economic divides become the outer or concrete manifestation of a divide that is also profoundly internal and relational.

While my family lived in Nairobi, my wife and I were involved in communities at the very opposites of the social spectrum. While so much of my world focused on Kibera and similar informal settlements, Anita's ministry revolved around the cathedral and the small expatriate community who, in Nairobi, tended to live in one of three large suburbs. We would joke with each other that we carried in our heads very different A to Z's of the city. Our geographies of Nairobi were almost unrecognizable to the other. The worlds we moved among seldom met, other than in the quiet evenings when we sat together and shared our day over a cup of coffee, bringing people and places into the same space only in our conversation.

The reality of these separate geographies is borne out in the way people can live a lifetime in a city and yet only relate to specific areas of it. In our mental geographies, the city shrinks to the size of the social world we inhabit. Barriers of fear, ignorance, prejudice, or the sense of simply not belonging there isolate areas of the city from our experience, reducing the diversity and complexity of urban life into something more manageable but significantly less vibrant and interesting.

This sense of living in separate worlds is brilliantly explored in David "Tosh" Gitonga's gritty film *Nairobi Half Life*. In it, the central character Mwas migrates from his rural home to pursue his dream of becoming an actor. Instead, he finds himself dragged into a life of brutality and crime. Yet while his life descends into chaos, he clings to the dream that brought him to the city and tries to hold on to a small acting role at the Phoenix Theatre. The two disparate worlds in which he finds himself finally enter each other's orbits as his anguished stage character cries out to the audience, "It is a choice to look or to look away."

But what happens when we decide not to look away, when we opt to move beyond the boundaries of a divided city? The process of building relationships across these divides and entering worlds that may be very different or unfamiliar to our own presents its own challenges.

Identifying the God-Complexes

One challenge in building healthy relationships across divided communities can be seen in what Bryant Myers (1999) describes as the God-complexes of the non-poor. It is an easy position to fall into when those from more privileged areas of a city seek to develop helping relationships with their less affluent neighbors. It is evidenced when we make ourselves authorities and experts in the lives and experiences of others. We enter communities with a sense that we can solve problems and make a difference, unaware that in reality we are the learners and even the ones most in need of change. It is not simply an aspect of individual relationships. Mission organizations, churches, and NGOs working in urban slums can frequently find themselves in this position.

Kibera was the constant venue of choice of international evangelists, yet I wonder how many considered what might be learned from this community about what it truly means to live by faith in Christ. NGOs entered with solutions to every kind of problem but perhaps were slow to recognize the innovative skills that had created and sustained the community. For my own part, I was forced to examine my sense of surprise when individuals and communities who had received training through the Centre for Urban Mission went on to demonstrate ways of using skills and information that went beyond anything any of us had envisaged. They understood their context better than we did.

Our attempts to develop certain training materials required a constant return to the drawing board as we discovered that expert solutions didn't always work and those developed and generated locally did. Our economic empowerment training program was just one example of training materials that were eventually completely rewritten from the experience of learning with and from local communities. Similarly, most of the course outlines and materials I carefully developed in the early years of the Centre were rapidly abandoned or significantly modified by members of staff who shared in and understood more deeply the communities in which we worked. We need to recognize within ourselves our frequent resistance to such processes. Sometimes it is easier to observe the signs of these complexes in others than in ourselves.

Sometimes the realities of these God-complexes come into the open if the right kind of space can be created to bring churches and church leaders together. Visits to the Warehouse, a ministry of churches in Cape Town, suggested they had a particular gift for this. Through monthly meetings, they created safe environments where church leaders could openly and confidently engage with one another with a level of trust that ensured that more difficult issues could be discussed and explored. In one meeting, I heard the pastor of a Pentecostal church in a very affluent, largely white suburb talking about the challenge of building relationships with pastors in the townships. For him, the primary stumbling block in relationships was the way conversations seemed to revolve around finance and the expectation of funds flowing from the wealthier churches to the townships. His deepest frustration was that he felt the relationships were not genuine, but simply a means to another end. I could sense he was both saddened and frustrated by the lack of progress in building what he would feel were real partnerships in mission and ministry.

The next person to speak was Zoleka, a Pentecostal pastor from one of the townships. She too expressed her sadness and frustration in the failure of these partnerships. She went on to talk about how many of the affluent suburban churches would want to visit them to do training, run courses, preach, and teach. The material might be excellent, but they would never be invited in return to teach or preach in the churches of those who visited them. At one point she said, "They don't see that we have something to teach them." For her, the deepest crisis was in the very understanding of these relationships. They seemed to be built upon a deception that equates possession of material resources and social advantage with spiritual maturity—even though Jesus indicated the very reverse.

We so easily assume economic and social status somehow convey spiritual depth and insight. Mission so often seems to be an activity flowing from the economically privileged to the economically poor. Sometimes our best and good intentions reinforce structures of relationships that need to be more critically examined and reconfigured.

From Myers, we learn that if we want to address the structural dimensions of urban poverty and marginalization, we must engage with the critical factor of relationships. Spatial injustice and the inequity of profound economic disparity cannot be addressed in isolation from the relationships in which they are lived out.

Creating a New Kind of Space

We began by looking at the realities of social and economic division and the gaps that provide the context for much of Jesus's teaching in Luke's Gospel. We have seen how in many respects these gaps mirror some of the realities of contemporary urban life and of a world that, in economic terms, appears to be moving ever further apart. But we are still left with the question of how we engage with these gaps. What does it mean to live faithfully in a world marked by such depths of division?

There are no easy answers to that question, but it cannot be enough merely to recognize the gaps and highlight their presence. We must explore what it might mean to enter them and to walk in them and in that sense to defy and resist them. Yet Jesus takes us a step further. His path is not one that merely overrides the social divisions and conventions of his day. He does not simply move between worlds accommodating himself to the people he encounters. Instead, he enters into the divided spaces in order to redeem them. He creates new possibilities for hope and transformation in relationships that have been marked by exclusion and marginalization. He creates a whole new space where as people encounter him they encounter one another in a new way, too.

Chapter 10
Redeeming the Gaps

His descent into our lowliness is the supreme expression of his power.

--Gregory of Nyssa

Another Possible World

In Nairobi, there is a popular poster that consists of two images of the city. One is called the Nairobi we want. It portrays a green, clean city with smiling people of all ages moving about freely and securely. It is marked by adequate housing and safe and rewarding employment. If Nairobi were to market itself to the world, this would be the image it would like to present. The other picture is called the Nairobi we have. This is a deeply pessimistic portrait of the city marked by pollution, insecurity, unsanitary housing, and exploitative employment. It is unquestionably overly negative, but it does portray a sense of people's longing for a different kind of city, a different experience of urban life.

Sometimes at the Centre for Urban Mission we would invite our students to take passages from Scripture, particularly from Isaiah, and rewrite them in ways that allow them to reenvision their own communities, prophetically reimagining their parts of the city in the light of God's redemptive purposes for his creation. Students would spend time together reading passages such as Isaiah 65, with his vision of a new heaven and a new earth, and then ask themselves what that vision would look like if it were spoken out of the realities of their own communities. The results of that imagination were often profoundly moving, as students gave voice not only to the desolation and injustice they saw around them, but also to the hopes and aspirations that began to take a more concrete form in their minds and imaginations. The exercise was important. While we need to hear words like repentance and hope, we also need to figure out what they look like in our lives, on our street, and in our communities. We need to give some form of material expression to that hope that we have within us.

That process of reimagining communities can only take us so far. It still leaves us with the critical question of how we move from where we are to those places that more clearly evidence God's purpose for his creation. It is one thing to develop a sense of a new destination; it is another thing to figure out how to get there.

In Luke, we can identify three aspects of Jesus's ministry and teaching that provide pointers as to how we might move toward that different kind of future. They involve the practice of economic discipleship, radical inclusion, and subversive hospitality. It is in these dimensions of Jesus's ministry that we see him creating a new community around himself that stands in stark contrast to the social and religious world he moved in.

In exploring these three areas of Jesus's ministry, we begin with the one who not only pointed towards Jesus, but in many respects anticipates these very aspects of his ministry. Enter John the Baptist.

Anticipating the Coming of the King

The opening verses of Luke 3 introduce us to a world dominated by powerful forces centered on Imperial Rome. When Luke unveils the ministry of John the Baptist, he begins by locating it against the backdrop of the most powerful figures of his day: the Emperor Tiberius and his Judean Governor; the sons of Herod the Great, who were ruling provinces of their father's now divided kingdom as client states of Rome; and the imperially appointed priesthood.

The list of names are not only there to provide us with a date for the start of John's ministry, but also to tell a story of political oppression and human misery (N.T. Wright, 2004, p. 32). It is as if the political, economic, and religious forces of the day had come together in an unholy alliance that served only to further alienate and subdue the people of the land. In the previous verse (Luke 2:52), Jesus has been introduced as the one who has grown in favor with God and humanity. The same could not be said of the names that followed. But amid the moral and spiritual wilderness of Israel's political and religious leadership, Luke announces the all-important words, "The word of the Lord came to John, son of Zechariah."

It was this longing to hear what God was saying in the midst of the uncertainties and oppression of their day that must have drawn the people to the message of John. It may be hard to see why a wild-looking preacher, dressed in camel's hair and roaming the area around the River Jordan would be such a crowd puller, but clearly John the Baptist struck a chord with a disillusioned people looking for answers.

Of course, John was not the only one to offer a word to God's people in the midst of national crisis. There were other voices and other possibilities available to the crowds that followed him. For many it must have been hard to know where to turn. Do you opt out like the Essenes, retreating into the desert and form a more holy and true community, preparing for the end-time? Do you follow the line of the Pharisees and focus on your personal purity, strictly adhering to a set of rules that leave you justified, at least in your own eyes, and demonstrate your distinctiveness from the world around you? Do you join political movements, such as those who became known as the Zealots, and push for radical political change and an overthrow of the whole system? Do you compromise with the system and try to turn it to your own benefit as the tax collectors did so effectively? In light of the options, John's message of repentance and the forgiveness of sins seems unpromising, focusing as it does on the sins of the people themselves and not on the powers that surround and oppress them. It certainly does not seem designed to garner the wave of popular support that accompanied his ministry.

Those who heard John's words, responded to them, and were plunged beneath the waters of the River Jordan stepped onto the river bank with their own questions. They had participated in this symbolic act but were troubled with the more concrete questions that followed. What does it mean to live this life that is marked by a radical U-turn and to live out the repentance their baptism signified? It was the simple question: What should we do? (Luke 3:10, 12, 14). It is a question that is repeated down the generations. What does it mean to live this new life? What does it look like? What does it ask of us in our daily living?

Like John the Baptist's audience, Christians are faced with various possibilities as we both confront the problems of our own age and try to anticipate a different future. As we think about the world we live in, or the towns and cities we inhabit, we may sense the same need for a radical U-turn in our world. But how do we begin to embrace that in our lives?

Perhaps the options are not so different from those of John's day. We can take the path of the Essenes and retreat into our spirituality, searching for personal holiness in a corrupt world. Like the Pharisees of Jesus's day, we can become ever more religious, seeking by a constant keeping of rules to demonstrate to ourselves and others that we are different from the word around us. Alternatively, like Zealots we can immerse ourselves in radical social and political activism. Leslie Newbiggin famously commented that the project of bringing heaven down to earth always results in bringing hell up from below (Newbiggin, as cited by Yancey, 1997, p. 234).

Finally, and perhaps more commonly, we slip into a more or less acceptable compromise with the things we cannot change, so that we increasingly conform to the lifestyles and values of the world around us. In this sense, we lose our anticipation of a different world as we increasingly conform and adapt ourselves to the way things are. We may not descend to the corrupt opportunism of the tax collector, but we can still share their ability to profit from political and economic systems that we would be hard-pressed to defend. These models of Essene, Pharisee, Zealot, or tax collector may not reliably capture the complexities of our own experience, but the inclination towards retreat, legalism, radicalism, and compromise seem to be evident in the church in every generation, including our own. If we are to move beyond these default positions, we need to consider what other options are open to us.

Practicing Economic Discipleship

The burning question on the lips of those who experienced John's baptism is intensely practical: What should we do? Three times the question is asked and by three different groups. First the question is put by the crowd, then by the tax collectors, and finally by the soldiers. Interestingly, the last two groups—tax collectors and soldiers—are those who perhaps find themselves most compromised by the existing political order. Luke tells us the crowd was looking for answers to two fundamental questions. The first centers on how they should live and what they should now do, while the second, unspoken, focuses on who John is, and implied with that, who they should follow.

There is a story that goes as follows:

A bishop visits one of his clergy in a poor rural parish. He is impressed with the ministry he sees but decides to put the rural clergyman to a simple test. "Pastor," he asks, "If you had two cars, what would you do?" Without a moment's thought, the pastor replies, "I would keep one and give away the other." "Good," the bishop says, "What if you had two motorbikes?" The pastor repeats his answer with increased confidence. He would keep one and give away the other. The bishop goes on, "What if you had two cows?" The pastor smiles, looks at his solitary cow and announces that he would give away the second cow.

Finally the bishop asks, "And what if you had two goats?"
The pastor suddenly becomes agitated. "Bishop, that is not
fair—you know I have two goats!"

When the people ask John what they should do, they are effectively
asking what it means to bear fruit befitting repentance. They are asking
for a clearer indication of what this looks like in the circumstances of
their own lives. John's answer takes us straight to the conclusion of the
bishop's questioning of his pastor and points to the very things that are
within their capacity to do. If you have two cloaks, give to someone who
doesn't have one, and the same with your food, share what you have. His
responses to the tax collectors and the soldiers are similar, and each time
they focus on the economic life of his hearers. Don't take what is not
due to you and don't practice corruption by way of extortion and
blackmail. Be content with what you have. The point of the instruction
is in its elementary nature—small, simple items that improve the
welfare of others (Foster, 1981, p. 38).

John's message to them is clear: a life of true repentance is marked
by both generosity and justice. The first thing these new converts are
instructed in is economic discipleship. How they use their wealth, their
stewardship of their possessions, and how they conduct their business
and economic life will be a sound measure of their renewal and
repentance. When faced with the question, "What should we do?" John
could have pointed them in any number of directions. Given the
political background of the day, we might have expected John to offer
very different advice to the tax collectors and the soldiers. Both careers
alienated them from the people and aligned them with oppressive and
unjust systems. No doubt the Essenes and Pharisees would have advised
them to turn their backs on this life of worldly compromise, and
Zealots would have wanted them actively to oppose the very worlds to
which they had belonged. John advocates for neither response. He tells
them to abandon greed and practice justice, integrity, and contentment
in the places they find themselves. We should not underestimate, given

the circumstances of the day, just what a challenging prospect that would have been.

The challenge is no less easy to implement in our day. How do we read John's encouragement to share food when in the United Kingdom it is reported that households throw away the equivalent of up to 24 meals per month. The figure for the United States is similar. What changes would I need to make to my wardrobe if I were to literally follow the injunction that anyone who has two shirts should share with those who have none? Of course John is speaking rhetorically. He is using hyperbole to bring home a central point that a life lived in anticipation of the one who is to come would be a life marked by extravagant generosity and a willingness to make personal sacrifice in response to the needs of another.

The problem lies not in the ownership of more than one shirt or in having a reasonably well-stocked pantry, but in the clinging to what we have in the face of another's need. Equally, there is a calling to a lifestyle that "travels light" because it is lived in anticipation of journeying with one who challenges us to abandon everything that hinders us from following him. It is a call to a lifestyle that will, in the words of Gregory of Nyssa, cling only to what is necessary.

Living out a generous and uncluttered life is far from straightforward, but it is not beyond our reach and is central to our discipleship. For some of us it inevitably requires a much more honest and critical look at our lifestyles and the values that sustain them. We may have to reappraise what we really consider to be necessary to our lives and what might be the excess baggage that ultimately impedes our following of Christ.

We may wonder why John chooses to highlight the economic dimension of his followers. Like the prophets before him, he could have instructed the people in keeping the Sabbath and shunning idolatry. Yet John seems to concentrate on this one area of people's lives. He has not adopted an easy path for himself, and he is not one of those preachers who reassures his audience with the words they want to hear. His life is one of uncompromising honesty that will ultimately lead to his death. In answering their question, John addresses his followers in the area of life that is simultaneously easy to comprehend and yet profoundly demanding to implement. Practice generosity and justice. These are not arbitrary values or a particular bias from a man who appears to have abandoned all worldly comforts. Like the prophets before him, he is instructing the people to imitate, in the practicalities of their lives, the very nature of a just and generous God. Micah says God requires us to do justice, to love mercy, and to walk humbly with our God (Mic 6:8). John tells his followers what this might look like.

Yet his message does not stop there. The heart of his message is that this repentance, evidenced in generosity and justice, is lived out in anticipation of and in preparation for the one who is to come.

Jesus and Economic Discipleship

It would be nice to think that somehow following Jesus is not, for us at least, tied up with John the Baptist's advice on economic discipleship. If John is the last of the prophets leading up to Jesus, and if in Jesus a new era has begun, then perhaps a new set of instructions applies. Unfortunately, phrases from Jesus suggest he and John were on the same page. In Luke 6:30, he says, "Give to everyone who asks you." In Luke 11:41, he says, "Give what is inside the dish to the poor." In Luke 12:33, he says, "Sell your possessions and give to the poor." In Luke 18:22, he says, "Sell everything you have and give to the poor." These themes run through the whole of Scripture. Our God is a God of generosity and justice and so are those who follow him. If we want to consider how that is to play out in our lives, we may want to look at how Jesus models that message in his life and ministry.

At the end of Luke 9, Jesus is walking along the road when a would-be disciple declares he will follow Jesus wherever he goes. Jesus is on his way to Jerusalem, and his disciples have been debating among themselves who will gain the greatest personal benefit from following him there (Luke 9:46–48). Perhaps this individual sees a similar opportunity to get in on the act. Jesus's response seems sharp and anything but encouraging, "Foxes have holes and birds of the air have nests, but the Son of Man has no place to lay his head" (Luke 9:58). Those following him in pursuit of personal gain would need to look again at whom they were following. Jesus modeled a life that demonstrated a radical detachment from material wealth and possession. He offers the enquirer the possibility of following him, while spelling out the nature of that path in terms of the realities of his life. In sending out the 12 in Luke 9 and the 72 in Luke 10, he similarly sends them out as he is, devoid of personal wealth and radically vulnerable.

There is a danger that we may begin to make special pleading in relation to how we perceive the relevance of Jesus's instructions to our own discipleship. One form this takes sees these verses as applying almost exclusively to those involved in global or cross-cultural mission —those who get on the plane or the boat headed for cultures and countries other than their own. By applying the verses in this way, we manage to place on the backs of our sisters and brothers an obligation we might be unwilling to carry ourselves, and at the same time conveniently ensure the two passages do not apply to the vast majority of the church whose mission is lived out in their local context.

Of course, these verses do have a profound relevance for those engaged in global mission and particularly to those who move from highly developed Western economies to those of developing nations. If we are called to enter that Fourth World, which Castells reminds us exists in every nation and particularly in global cities, then wealth and possession will easily become a burden and an obstacle to our relationships with others. There is a growing awareness that Western models of mission, which carry with them the perpetuation of Western lifestyles, are unsustainable as well as unbiblical (Harries, 2012). Jesus's instruction to his disciples presents a very particular challenge to our understanding of mission in global cities. In places that are by definition centers of wealth and opportunity, lifestyles—if you have the resources

—become more obviously a matter of choice. Where we locate ourselves and what form of lifestyle we adopt are difficult decisions that inevitably draw us closer or leave us increasingly detached from those at the margins of the city.

However, the emphasis in the passage is not on cross-cultural mission. The 12 and the 72 are sent to the towns and villages where Jesus himself would later go (Luke 10:1). They were involved in mission within their local cultural context. In this sense, the passages are applicable to all engaged in mission, whether in their immediate context or elsewhere in the world. The call to sit lightly towards possessions and to become radically vulnerable for the sake of living and proclaiming the Kingdom applies to the church as a whole. Jesus was not giving basic guidelines for a short mission trip. He was inviting his followers to model the Kingdom they were to proclaim by modeling his lifestyle.

Radical Inclusion

One of the most fantastic things about the church is its rich diversity and the very different ways individuals, communities, and cultures have developed to express what it means to be a community of people who follow Jesus. Such diversity will always be a cause for celebration of the wonder of God's creation revealed in our humanity. But in the rightful task of celebrating diversity we also risk the possibility of baptizing division. It is so easy to sell our birthright as the church, abandoning our true vocation and inheritance, in exchange for diminished visions that leave us little more than chaplains to a divided city and world.

Against this background, we see Jesus representing something very different in his dealings with those on various sides of the divisions of his day. Most particularly, we see it in the way he deals with the gaps between insiders and outsiders and between those who form the center and those who form the periphery. Jesus demonstrates an inclusiveness in his approach to others, which is radical because it overturns the very conventions of belonging, both socially and religiously. Jesus takes us to the roots of what it means to include others in ways that demonstrate God's welcome and unrestricted hospitality.

The inclusiveness that Jesus embodies is radical in two ways. First, his inclusiveness is radical in terms of who is included. In Luke's Gospel we are constantly reminded, in both the parables and ministry of Jesus, that those most marginalized and most excluded are those who appear central to his concern. The poor, the crippled, the blind, and the lame become invited guests of the heavenly banquet. Jesus is constantly drawing in those whom the world might otherwise exclude. But perhaps more importantly, we see the radical nature of Jesus's inclusiveness in terms of how people are included. Those at the margins are not simply included in the circle, permitted to form part of the larger crowd, and given a space. Rather, they enter in a way that reconfigures the community surrounding him and questions the very patterns of inclusion and exclusion that have set them aside. Those excluded enter the space created by Jesus as the invited guests, the models of discipleship, the greatest in the Kingdom of heaven. In the community that Jesus seems to be creating, you have to walk to the margins in order to discover the center.

Crossing Boundaries

A story is told of the retirement party held by Nelson Mandela when he left office as president of South Africa. The event was held in a smart hotel at the Cape Town Waterfront. Typical of the man, but probably not of most presidential retirement functions, all his staff were invited, including the domestic and gardening staff. Inevitably, the party had a strong security presence, particularly at the entrance to the hotel, in anticipation of his arrival. In the final moments before the official limousine arrived at the venue, a rather tired old man in torn oil-stained overalls found himself in the wrong place at the wrong time. The security personnel rapidly tried to shoo him away just as the metallic blue Mercedes-Benz pulled up outside the hotel. Out stepped Nelson

Mandela who then proceeded to walk straight over to the man in the overalls and grasp him by the hand. "How are you?" he enquired.

Reading through Luke's Gospel, we repeatedly see the way Jesus cuts across the gaps and divides of his day. He does not opt for a middle way by gravitating toward an acceptable compromise. He refuses to be captured by the conventions and prejudices that separate people from each other. This is evident in the way he allows access to people who others might turn away. In Luke 5, we see him reach out to touch the man with leprosy. We see it in the way he is criticized for keeping the company of sinners and tax collectors. Yet he also eats with scribes and Pharisees and the religious and social elite of his day.

We can also see how the stories Jesus tells challenge conventions and attitudes that create barriers between people. When an expert in the law questions Jesus on who is his neighbor (Luke 10:29), he is not simply trying to corner Jesus. He is reflecting a deeply held concern within contemporary Judaism: Who is and who is not included in the community of God's people? Yet the parable Jesus offers in response takes us deeper into that question. We are invited not only to consider the question of who is my neighbor, but also to grapple with what loving our neighbor looks like in practice. Jesus delves into the difficult area of the tension between being a good neighbor and retaining boundaries of purity. What happens if the Levitical requirements in relation to personal purity appear to conflict with the command to love one's neighbor? Jesus steps into these waters with his story of the Good Samaritan.

In the parable, we have to ask what motivates the priest and the Levite to pass by the man who lies in the road. Is it insecurity and fear that make them wish to move on quickly, or even the simple fear of the implications of becoming involved? However, their occupations suggest that religion is playing a critical part in this story. It seems as if the very practice of religion can become a barrier to good neighborliness. The concern for ritual purity, which would be compromised by the blood of the injured man, causes the priest and Levite to maintain their distance.

Yet Jesus shows that the practice of loving our neighbor will take priority over these carefully drawn boundaries. Jesus pushes the boundaries one step further by casting a Samaritan as the hero of the piece. In one carefully drawn story, he moves across boundaries created by fear, religious dogma, and historic antipathy to redefine what it means to be the loving neighbor (Moore, 2011, p. 205).

We also see Jesus crossing boundaries in the way he brings together people who might not otherwise encounter one another. At times that can have uncomfortable results. It is the presence of Jesus that brings a woman with a dubious reputation into the home of Simon, a Pharisee (Luke 7:36–50). Simon's discomfort at the intimate and physical way she expresses her adoration of Jesus is evident. But the reality is that the presence of Jesus in the home brought their two worlds into the same room. The same is true of Luke 14, where the man with dropsy finds himself in the midst of a meal where the invited guests are religious legal experts. Their worlds might never normally intersect, but in the presence of Jesus they find themselves sharing the same space. Jesus's meals have the function not of creating distinctions, but of bridging them and including people (Moxnes, 1988, p. 88).

Sadly, there is no indication these encounters brought a lasting change in relationships between the characters who found themselves in Jesus's presence. In Luke 7, we see Jesus urging Simon to escape from his prejudices about the sinful woman and open his eyes to what she might teach him about forgiveness, love, and devotion. Her actions reveal that she is the one who discerns most clearly who Jesus is, although she undoubtedly has none of Simon's learning. The presence of Jesus has brought together two radically opposing worlds. The encounter could have changed them both, but one senses only the woman went away changed.

A Community Where the Blind Will Lead

The blind beggar in Luke 18, whom Mark identifies as Bartimaeus, gives us a good picture of what radical inclusion looks like. This

135

encounter with Jesus follows a section of his teaching where it seems those who are thought to be nearest the Kingdom of God are the furthest away and those who are far turn out to be near. In Luke 18:7, in the telling of the parable of the persistent widow, Jesus declares God will bring about justice for his chosen ones who cry out to him day and night. But who are these chosen ones? The answer to that seems surprising. In the healing of the 10 men with leprosy in Luke 17, it is the one Samaritan in the group, returning to give thanks for his healing, who is told his faith has made him well. Later, in the same chapter, we are told that in the coming of the Kingdom of God it is those who keep their life who will lose it and those who lose their life who will keep it. This upside-down view of the world is made clearer in Luke 18, where we see the tax collector, and not the righteous Pharisee, is justified by God (Luke 18:9–14). Meanwhile, the children will inherit the Kingdom of God (Luke 18:16) while the rich ruler (Luke 18:18–30), in sad fulfillment of Mary's song, walks away empty.

In the verses immediately before the healing of the blind man, we encounter Jesus's disciples in deep confusion. They have left everything to follow Jesus, and yet at this critical point in their journey they are left to ponder the most basic question: Who on earth can be saved? In answer, Jesus directs their thinking toward his own suffering, death, and resurrection, but the meaning of his words is totally lost on the very people who were closest to him. As Gregory the Great noted, the disciples have discovered and learned much on their journey with Jesus, but there are certain things, even very plain things, to which they remain blind (Gregory the Great, as cited by Jeffrey, 2012, p. 223).

In the next chapter, we approach the last recorded miracle in the Gospel before the resurrection of Jesus. Within these events, we are invited to ponder what it means truly to see and follow Jesus. The answer appears to be found in two highly unlikely characters, a blind beggar and a tax collector. Their radical inclusion in the company of those who follow Jesus is designed to show us the nature of true discipleship.

Chapter 11
The Alternative Disciples

With each new era, each new situation of poverty and oppression, God calls people forth in a new way.

--Jean Vanier

One Sunday, I drove to church in Kibera. It is only a short distance from our home, and I could have taken a matatu (public transport vehicle), but on this occasion I had a keyboard to transport. Arriving close to a suitable parking spot, I heard a voice shout out in my direction, "Hey mzungu!" (white European). My heart sank. I knew what was coming. Sure enough, as I began to park, my self-appointed parking assistant arrived on the scene. A youth in an orange T-shirt, which announces a particular political affiliation, was calling out to me.

I can usually deal with these situations with humor, but somehow not on this occasion. As the young man began to direct my car into the spot I was quite capable of parking in unaided, I reversed in the direction of another space behind me. Within moments the young man was visible in my rear mirror directing me again towards that same spot. The moment I parked I knew I would be informed that he was now protecting my car, in anticipation of a small fee. Frustration took over, and I changed gear again and headed forward to find another space, which gave me the opportunity to park and get on my way without being disturbed. I quickly got out and headed for church feeling irrational levels of annoyance at the simple event.

Arriving at church, I discovered the preacher would not be coming, or more accurately the preacher had arrived—me. Feeling unprepared in every sense, I sat down and tried to work out the source of my anger and frustration. I had been coming to this part of Kibera for more than 10 years. I felt some sense of belonging here, some connection, which made me more than just the *mzungu*—the white man. But to the youth I was just a *mzungu*, a possible source of easy income.

I began to reflect on the youth. We hadn't really spoken, beyond my efforts to resist his attention. He too had a name and unquestionably a far more significant history and rootedness in this place than I had. But I had not acknowledged it and had resolutely avoided conversation. In my frustration, he was just a youth out to make a quick buck at my expense—not a person to engage with meaningfully.

It wasn't that I was unconcerned about young people in Kibera. In both the church and the Centre for Urban Mission, we were actively involved in initiatives to support young people in education, employment, and Christian discipleship. But perhaps there are moments when we seem ready to embrace concerns while simultaneously insulating ourselves from their human faces. Then we have to make the conscious effort to reorient our lives, take a detour, and encounter the person who, uninvited, has just stepped into our world. That morning might have been very different if either of us had found the grace and courage to move beyond those labels of youth and *mzungu* to the places where strangers meet, eyes are opened, and the potential for change unfolds along the road.

Creating a Different Kind of Space

In the closing verses of Luke 17, we find Jesus on the road heading toward Jericho. It seems there is quite an entourage with him as they approach the city. Beyond the boundaries of the city, there is the all-too-familiar sight of beggars plying their trade, or at least making their appeal, to the travelers entering and leaving Jericho. At least one of these beggars is blind. A crowd moves with Jesus in the midst of the road, the beggar sits at its margins, away from the crowd, not a follower, hardly an observer. He occupies a liminal space of rejection by society (Arbuckle, 2010, p. 155).

There is no elaboration of the economic gap beyond the essential reality that this is a roadside beggar seeking to make an income from the passing crowds. Where the gap is most evident is at the level of relationship. Unlike in the Lazarus story, this man is not ignored, but instead the effort is made to silence him. The crowd will tell him who is the source of all the commotion, but they are deeply reluctant to include him among those who accompany Jesus. The phrase, "Jesus of Nazareth is passing!" might just have easily been, "Jesus of Nazareth is passing you by." But that is a notion Jesus won't entertain.

In sharp contrast to the Lazarus story, we see the agency of the blind beggar; he will not be silenced by the crowd. He cannot see, yet his cry to the Son of David, rather than to Jesus of Nazareth, suggests he may see more than those on the road. Echoing the words of the tax collector in the preceding parable (Luke 18:13), he cries out to Jesus for the very thing he knows Jesus can give. Ironically, this cry also echoes the appeal of the rich man to Abraham (Luke 16: 24). The blind man cries out in his poverty for the very thing that the rich man failed to either give or receive—mercy.

Jesus's response is interesting. He suspends his journey and calls for the blind man to be brought to him. Immediately the physical space between them, between those in the road and those at the roadside, is challenged. The blind man is brought into the heart of the crowd. While the crowd would seek to exclude him, Jesus himself invites him into his presence. Facing one another, Jesus asks, "What do you want me to do for you?" Again, this is a far cry from the passivity of Lazarus. The blind man is asked to exercise faith and give voice to the hope he has in Jesus. In contrast, the crowd has understood neither the Jesus they accompany nor the beggar they sought to silence.

While Jesus had announced in Nazareth that he had come to open the eyes of the blind, the crowd has effectively become the barrier to the very things Christ has come to do. The small gap between the roadside and the road is made impenetrable by his followers. They see their role as preserving the boundaries that will exclude the very ones for whom Jesus has come. It is as if they have become the self-appointed gatekeepers to a banquet whose favored guests—the poor, the crippled, the blind, and the lame—they seek to deter. They enter this gap, this space in the road, not in ways that overcome it, but in ways that create deeper distance and division. In this sense they too have become like the Pharisees. They have become the brokers not between the Torah, the Temple, and the people, but between Jesus and the world he has come to save. Like the Pharisees, instead of facilitating access, they have become the source of a deeper alienation and separation. They rebuke the beggar and command his silence. Yet Jesus will not allow this role. He demands a parting of the crowd and the creation of a different kind of space, where he and the beggar will meet on the road.

Jesus's response to the blind man is instant. He gives him the very thing the beggar has sought, his sight. It is the beggar's faith, a faith that overcame the resistance of Jesus's own followers, which brought his healing. It was faith that saw with far greater clarity than the crowd who Jesus was and what he had come to do. Again we see Bartimaeus's life in marked contrast to the passivity of Lazarus. The one who cries out from the roadside is the one who now shouts out praises in the street. The one who the crowd would have kept at the roadside is now the one who follows Jesus. In Luke 18:28, Peter reminded Jesus that the disciples have left everything to follow him. This man has left only his isolation and dependency, but by doing so he has become to the rest of the crowd an example of what it means to be a follower of Jesus. In the opening of an eye, he moves from the margin to the center of the community. His inclusion marks a conversion in the attitudes and faith of the crowd. Those who sought to exclude him find themselves caught up with him in praise of what God has done (Luke 18:43). The people's eyes have been opened, too.

Moving into Places of Exclusion

Moving between worlds in ways that radically include outsiders creates new possibilities in relationships that potentially change us and others. Yet that process also comes with real costs, which cannot be ignored. In the early years of starting the Centre for Urban Mission, our students on the three-year diploma program were almost exclusively pastors and evangelists who were already living and working in slums. However as the course became more widely known, we began to get applications from prospective students who lived in other contexts but had a sense of calling to mission in these parts of the city. Two such students were Moses and Simon Peter. At the time, they were both actively involved in ministry in a very lively church on the edge of Nairobi. After an interview, we offered them both a place, but we insisted they live in Kibera for the duration of the course.

It was about seven years before I discovered how costly that decision had been for Simon. Telling his story to a group of students, he described his first months in Kibera. One of the most difficult aspects of his initial time there had been the cries he continually heard from a child being regularly beaten by its mother. Walls in Kibera are made of plywood and iron sheet, so little is hidden or private. The cries of this child simply added another layer to the inner turmoil Simon was experiencing in adjusting to a very different sort of life in this community.

Finally, Simon took courage to confront the woman. I suspect he thought this would be a very difficult encounter. It wasn't. He discovered she made a small income frying fish. She was struggling as a single parent with a disabled daughter and was perhaps taking out some of her hurts and frustrations on the child. A conversation began. Simon began to buy his fish there and build a relationship. Later they would talk about other ways of disciplining the child that did not involve physical punishment. They remain friends eight years later.

In this unlikely relationship, Simon found his own sense of vocation and calling. When he finished the course, he continued to live in Kibera and worked with the local church, particularly in the area of ministry among vulnerable children. He now works with the Centre for Urban Mission heading up a children's ministry program. Reflecting on his experience, Simon later wrote:

> Kibera became God's mouthpiece that spoke to me about my ministry and life. In some sense people that I encountered in Kibera became God's spokespersons to me, and I think my refusal and denial of that fact made me struggle with urban mission for the first three years of my stay and study in Kibera. But when I saw Kibera people as God's spokesperson to me and accepted that fact then I began receiving some gifts from Kibera that have changed my life immensely.

What particularly strikes me in Simon's story is the way his own life was turned around by being among people at the margins. He later suggested his life had, in some ways, been redeemed by Kibera. When we seek to draw near to Christ, he often draws us into encounters with people whose life experience is radically different from our own but who may, if we are open to it, provide us with a deeper revelation of Christ and a richer sense of what it might mean to follow him. In this, we are never catalysts. A catalyst brings change within a chemical compound while it remains unchanged. Instead, these encounters radically change us as much as the people we encounter.

Cities create the opportunities for precisely these encounters because of the way they often draw together groups from varied social, cultural, economic, racial, and religious backgrounds. The question is what we do with those opportunities. The Pharisees in Luke 7 and Luke 14 would no doubt have been more comfortable to encounter Jesus within the confines of their own relationships and the boundaries of their social worlds. Jesus's presence among them seems to make that impossible. His crossing of boundaries will have implications for those who would be with him, whether they desire it or not. They try to create an exclusive table, but with Jesus present that seems like an unlikely outcome.

Subversive Hospitality

In looking at the practice of economic discipleship, we have seen Jesus challenging our attitudes to property and possession. In this regard, we are in some sense dealing with those things external to ourselves. Radical inclusion takes us further. It asks questions of our relationship with others, particularly those at the margins, challenging us to build community in ways that reflect the strangeness of God's Kingdom where the margins turn out to be the center. Subversive hospitality builds on that understanding of radical inclusion. It highlights the nature and boundaries of giving and receiving within those inclusive relationships.

We do not usually think of hospitality in terms that are subversive, and yet we see in the ministry of Jesus that the way he gives and receives hospitality causes deep offense. It leaves others feeling that some important boundaries have been breached or undermined. Jesus embodies hospitality in ways that not only ignore certain social and religious conventions, but that fundamentally challenge them. The story of Zacchaeus illustrates this particularly well.

In the Home of the Tax Collector

We are introduced to Zacchaeus as a chief tax collector. He is someone who is anything but at the economic margins. As chief tax collector, it is likely he got a percentage of all the local tax collectors' incomes, however it was acquired. He had possibly outbid his rivals to purchase this position from the Roman authorities (Patella, 2005, p. 123). Zacchaeus is a man of wealth, yet he is socially alienated. His alienation has an economic dimension to it, but is the alienation that comes from ill-gotten wealth, not from poverty. His name, derived from the Hebrew *zakkay*, means righteous one, but his occupation makes it sound deeply ironic. In the words of Michael Card (2010), he is a slimy good-for-nothing thief (p. 212). His role as a chief tax collector would suggest he is deeply implicated within the corrupt tax system of the Roman government. It is highly unlikely he could have risen to this level without a high degree of complicity.

Again in the story, the spatial, economic, and relational dimensions of alienation are evident and initially serve to separate him from Jesus. Like the blind beggar who precedes him, he desires to see Jesus but is unable to do so. He is handicapped by his size rather than by his eyesight, but like the blind man, his exclusion is primarily determined by the crowd. Those who are around Jesus represent the most significant obstacle to him encountering Jesus. It is not that Zacchaeus is consciously excluded or rebuked, but simply that Jesus's followers create a barrier he cannot penetrate. He is invisible to the crowd, and Jesus is invisible to him.

The spatial dimension of his alienation, reenacted by almost every Sunday school, is expressed in terms of Zacchaeus being away from the road and up the sycamore tree. He has placed himself in such a way that he is emphatically apart from the crowd but in a place where Jesus becomes visible. He is not inside this moving party making its way through the city, but like Lazarus at the rich man's gate he can look on and hope.

The relational dimension is again most evident. Perhaps for someone else the crowd would have created some space, but not for Zacchaeus. When Jesus breaks his journey for the second time and invites Zacchaeus to come down from the tree, Jesus confronts Zacchaeus's alienation and invites him to leave the isolation of the tree and enter with Jesus into the space of his home. At this point, the crowd expresses offense and seeks to reestablish Zacchaeus as the outsider. Jesus has gone to be the guest of a sinner, they cry. Jesus has crossed the boundary that divided Zacchaeus from the people. He has torn up the rulebook and created a new space where sinner and savior sit at the same table. He has, yet again, demonstrated a radical reversal of people's expectations.

In Zacchaeus's response to Jesus, we see the very fruits of repentance that John had preached about in Luke 3. Zacchaeus's actions stand in sharp contrast to those of the rich ruler of the previous chapter. The ruler asks what he must do to inherit eternal life, but then finds his attachments to material wealth leave him unable to follow Jesus. He is, in effect, impoverished by wealth. By contrast, Zacchaeus, having responded to Christ's invitation to enter his home, spontaneously gives away more than the law would ever have required of him in making restitution for ill-gotten gain. He embraces grace and mercy and demonstrates it in his response to others.

In *The Sacrifice of Africa*, the Ugandan theologian Emmanuel Katongole says Zacchaeus's encounter with Jesus is a meeting marked by both loss and gain. As a man of wealth and power, he must divest himself of the very things that separate him from others if he is to discover intimacy with Jesus, the crowds, and the new sense of community, justice, mission, and salvation that will flow from his action. Katongole describes this primarily as a letting-go of power and a relinquishing of protective distance. He says:

> He had to sacrifice the clear vision that being up on a tree provided and the 'power' that the vantage point provided him: the power of clear sight, and the power of seeing without being seen—a panopticon—which is the real meaning of power, of touching without being touched. He now had to come down and join the disorderly crowds and be seen and touched by them. (Katongole, 2011, p. 136)

It is here, as Zacchaeus loses his attachments to wealth and power, that Jesus will declare that salvation has come to this house "because this man, too, is a son of Abraham" (Luke 19:9). In that moment, we are taken back to John the Baptist and his warning that if God so wished he could raise sons of Abraham from the rocks of the River Jordan. To be a true child of Abraham is not simply a matter of lineage. It comes through bearing the fruit of true repentance. This was a lesson the rich man had failed to grasp in Luke 16 as he vainly makes his plea to Abraham. Ultimately, the individuals in Luke's Gospel who are specifically identified as the children of Abraham are a crippled woman (Luke 13:16) and a corrupt tax collector. Both share the experience of having their lives turned around by Jesus.

As Jesus declares salvation has come to Zacchaeus's home, we are reminded of the earlier question put to Jesus by his followers: "Who then can be saved?" (Luke 18:26). The answer is: Zacchaeus, a deeply corrupt (one presumes), highly wealthy tax collector who has just embraced mercy and grace. They can look at the evidence, see the fruit. Zacchaeus not only goes beyond the requirements of restitution, offering to repay four times what he has cheated people of, but determines to give away half of all his possessions to the poor. A reckless generosity is at work and an uninhibited response to grace. As a tax collector, Zacchaeus would have contractual obligations to the Roman authorities and would risk the confiscation of all his property, even being sold into slavery, if he were unable to fulfill those obligations (Patella, 2005, p. 123). Yet in the face of these odds, he practices a generosity that reflects the very nature of the one he has elected to follow.

If I were Jesus at this moment, I suspect I might have advised Zacchaeus to respond more carefully, less impulsively, less radically. Yet like the woman who poured the ointment on Jesus feet, Zacchaeus, forgiven much, displays an unfettered generosity, which is the very fruit of his repentance. His experience of salvation suggests something that is neither individualistic nor private. It is personal, yet has profound social consequences, as he shares his goods with the poor. It is a transformation of life that begins in his own person, yet extends to his household and from there to the poor and to those he has cheated. His salvation has personal, domestic, social, and economic dimensions (Craddock, 1990, p. 220). Katongole takes this further and sees a wider political implication in the story. He interprets it as an example of a theology of relocation, where change is understood to come, not from the exercise of power from the center, but from the divesting of power and wealth to the margins.

Receiving Hospitality

It is important to see that Jesus acts as one who both gives and receives hospitality. At one level, he acts subversively by entering into Zacchaeus's home. In a very public way, he receives the hospitality of one ostracized by others. As so often in the ministry of Jesus, his deepest offense is in allowing others to minister to him. He defies both the self-sufficiency that might be expected of the one who can, if he chooses, turn stones to bread, and the social and religious conventions of his day that would place him at a distance from the unclean, the sinner, and the despised. Whether Jesus is having his feet washed with the tears of a sinful woman or sharing a resurrection meal with those who have so far failed to see or recognize him (Luke 21), he receives with absolute grace the hospitality of others.

In Jesus, we see something fundamentally dignifying in receiving the hospitality of others. This is particularly true in contexts and cultures that place a premium value on hospitality. But to be entertained by the stranger, healed by the broken, fed by the hungry, anointed by the sinner, included by the excluded, and receive from the empty, are the marks of a subversive hospitality that will always recognize in the other what is to be received with grace and joy.

One of our organization's earliest failures in our relationship with the community came when we were asked to do some training for more than 100 students for a week. Uncertain how we could cater for so many on the charcoal stoves we used at the time, we arranged for the food to be cooked at the college and carried into Kibera in large containers. As a practical way of catering for a large group, it was effective. As a step toward deepening relationships with the community, it was a total and with hindsight, entirely predictable disaster. Within moments of the food arriving, we had a delegation of women at our door. They daily cooked maize, beans, and chapattis on the roadside leading to the Centre. Of course they were angry about not getting the business, but more fundamentally they were angry and astonished that we had not considered that they were perfectly capable of meeting our needs. We had walked past them every day but had not observed them as people with skills and opportunities who could contribute to the work we were doing. We had refused them the possibility of extending a form of hospitality to us. We did not make the same mistake again.

Giving Hospitality

In his encounter with Zacchaeus, Jesus is not only subversive in the way he receives hospitality, but also deeply subversive in the way he gives it. When he declares, "This man too is a child of Abraham," he is including into the fellowship and community of God's people a man whose very occupation marked him as a sinner and demanded his exclusion. The one who is undoubtedly hated by many in the community and perhaps seen by some as a traitor to his nation is affirmed by Jesus as belonging to the community of the faithful. Jesus's message that God's hospitality extends to Zacchaeus is a message the crowd is not ready to hear, perhaps because Jesus's words of inclusion mark a change in Zacchaeus's relationship with the God of their father Abraham and, by extension, with them as well.

In the very person of Jesus, the coming of the Kingdom of God will subvert and overturn the tables of this present world, and something as apparently innocent as hospitality becomes a demonstration and foretaste of that kingdom. We see this explicitly if we return to Luke 14, where a Pharisee entertains Jesus at a banquet.

Although the Pharisee lives in a social world that placed store in hospitality, he was unquestionably practicing entertaining instead of true hospitality. He invited Jesus to join a meal with guests who were from a similar social and economic status and background. When Jesus encourages him to invite the poor, the crippled, the blind, and the lame to share the meal, Jesus is pushing the boundaries from entertaining to hospitality, in which there is no expectation or perhaps even possibility of reciprocity. Jesus suddenly proposes a very different kind of feast, a meal in which the most marginalized of people find themselves sitting at table with the social and religious elite of the day. The boundaries of the old social order are to be subverted by a radical generosity in anticipation of the heavenly banquet where the poor of the earth become the invited guests.

People in materially poor communities are often far more open than the rich to reordering their lives or plans in ways that allow them to welcome and embrace the outsider. For those living at the economic margins, hospitality may form part of the very fabric of their survival. When life is tough, the generosity of others may be all they have to fall back on. In places like Kibera, showing hospitality to the stranger, the new urban migrant, the recently displaced, or the evicted can be part of the mechanisms that enable vulnerable communities to maintain a place in the city, however tenuous.

Hospitality is also a feature of many traditional societies. Hospitality to the stranger is a social imperative. Ghanan theologian Mercy Oduyoye describes hospitality as being inherent to being African. True hospitality is a rare gift in some societies, but a more common one in others. For some, it is virtually second nature to practice hospitality. "Hospitality is perceived and practiced by Africans as open-handed, instinctive and the most natural thing in the world" (as cited by Githogo, 2006).

While living in India, I attended a baptism of a child of a member of the congregation. Afterwards, people were invited into the home for lunch. The home was a small and simple two-roomed house. As was the custom, I removed my shoes at the door and found a place on the floor to sit while food was brought to me. At one point, someone entered the room I didn't recognize and who didn't seem dressed for the occasion.

He walked in and sat down. The host came and served him a meal that he ate quietly, and then he left. "Who was that?" I asked once the person had left. The host had no idea, but someone entered his home, and he was happy for the visitor to share in the meal!

I suspect that experience would be repeated in any of the homes I knew in Kibera. To be visited is a blessing. Like many others, I have struggled with the experience of staying with a family and finding that I am to sleep on the bed while the rest of the family will occupy the floor. Hospitality dislocates us in some way in order that the other may be located. On another occasion, I visited family in Kibera on the birthday of a child who shared my name. I brought a cake. I should not have been surprised when the cake was promptly cut into small cubes and taken out of the door to be shared with all the children in the street. It was a natural cultural instinct that seems utterly unremarkable to families in some parts of the world, but far from normal in others. There is an openhandedness in hospitality that does not carefully discriminate those with whom we share.

Hospitality inevitably involves some form of risk, simply because we do not have control of events. As John Caputo (2013) remarks in his article "The Insistence of God: A Theology of Perhaps," "Hospitality means to say come in response to what is calling, and that may well be trouble."

While living in Bermondsey, we would often have homeless people calling at our door. They generally wanted some food or occasionally needed us to arrange night shelter accommodations. One such visitor arrived on a cold evening when it was too late to make alternative arrangements. Eventually, with much trepidation, we agreed he could stay the night with us. Sitting in our lounge he began to explain that he had recently come out of prison, but he was not like some of the very bad people that he had encountered there. "What were you in prison for?" we asked cautiously. "Manslaughter," he responded. That night we slept, somewhat sporadically, with a chair up against our bedroom door. Our fears were unfounded, and he left quietly after breakfast.

Hospitality requires openness to the stranger and perhaps, at times, to the attendant risk that goes with it.

Western values, which emphasize privacy, order, and planning, make it much harder to exhibit generous openness that allows our worlds to be invaded by others or to spontaneously seize the moments that invite us to enter into another's world. Yet divisions are often overcome through such actions. Henri Nouwen (1986) said:

> Hospitality means primarily the creation of free space where the stranger can enter and become a friend instead of an enemy. Hospitality is not to change people, but to offer them space where change can take place. It is not to bring men and women over to our side, but to offer freedom not disturbed by dividing lines. (p. 76)

If we are to ask what forms the greatest barriers to this subversive hospitality, we will have to confront the complexities of our lifestyles and the attachments we form to the things and places that surround our lives. So often our lifestyle can separate us from the poor. The basic reality of where we live in the context of a divided city can mean our lives seldom intersect with those at the margins. Sometimes it is the way we live that creates the barriers. We begin to see the spaces we occupy as places to preserve and protect more than places to welcome and receive.

Creating a New Space

In the stories of Bartimaeus and Zacchaeus, we see narratives played out in ways that are the complete opposite of the parable of the rich man and Lazarus. In both cases there is a gap, a division that separates people from one another and separates them from Jesus. Yet while the parable of Luke 16 leaves us with the hopelessness of lives drifting ever further apart, in the accounts of the blind man and Zacchaeus we see these gaps not narrowed but utterly transformed. Jesus seemingly creates new spaces, where lives are turned around and the possibility of new relationships unfolds. The individuals enter into a relationship with him, yet their relationship with others is also radically reconfigured. The one who was told to be silent becomes the one who leads others in the praise of God. The deceitful tax collector becomes the friend of the poor.

In the most central and crucial journey of Jesus's entire life, his final movement toward Jerusalem, Jesus allows his path to be diverted and to enter into the gap that separates people from himself and from the crowd. He then creates in that gap a redemptive space that not only changes the individuals, but reorders their social and economic relationships in ways that bring change in others. In this action of refusing the gaps, and cutting through the barriers of division and exclusion, Jesus creates new narratives, which are altogether different to the distorted world of the rich man and Lazarus.

Yet there is also a concerted resistance to the creation of this redemptive space, and sadly it comes from the very people who accompany Jesus along the way. Those who surround him become a barrier to shield him from those who seek him. Rather than being the servant who heads into the highways and byways to invite all and sundry to come in, the crowd creates for themselves the role of a regulator seeking to monitor and maintain the very boundaries that Jesus so patently disregarded.

Churches can similarly become exclusive communities. Like the priest and the Levite in the parable of the Good Samaritan, we find that the demands of maintaining boundaries and preserving some sense of purity and identity often override the demands of open hospitality to the stranger and the unloved. Rather than becoming windows through which the world might catch a clearer glimpse of grace, we become something altogether more opaque.

Bob Ekblad (2005), in his wonderful reading of the Scriptures amid the alienated and marginalized of United States society, among prisoners and illegal aliens, alludes to the way that in this dynamic of exclusion the church may not only mirror the processes of social exclusion in wider society but also legitimize them. He speaks of a dominant theology that sees God as a Border Patrol chief and the church as his deputies (p. 182). With this mind-set, the church does not simply create boundaries of exclusion that separate the marginalized from the liberating power of the Gospel, but also fosters a posture in which Christians give unquestioning support to laws and policies that further marginalize the immigrant, the unemployed, or those caught in descending spirals of addiction and crime. Yet as we ponder Jesus's encounter with a blind beggar and a corrupt tax collector, we see an altogether different picture: the possibility to create space and realize new narratives that embrace and include. Here, the impulse of grace overcomes the forces that would separate us from Christ and from those he calls the least of these, his brothers.

Chapter 12
Reimagining the City

The trouble with normal, is it always gets worse.

--Bruce Cockburn

A Tale of Two Cities

In the second half of Luke 19, Jesus and his disciples are on the final leg of a journey, climbing from Jericho to Jerusalem and toward the climax of the Gospel. In anticipation of this, Jesus tells the parable of the nobleman who goes off to be made king, in spite of the opposition of his future subjects. The story would have rung bells with Jesus's hearers, echoing as it did the events surrounding Archelaus, older brother of Herod Antipas. He went to Rome to be made king but was followed by a delegation of Judeans who did not want him. But as the parable unfolds, we begin to see that this is not a political satire. Rather, it becomes clear that the unwanted king who returns is in fact God, returning to his people. Israel's hope and expectation is finally being fulfilled—God the King will return to Israel, but not in the manner they expect.

This parable and the triumphant entry into the city parallel each other. The king returns, yet his return will be cause for both celebration and tears, for judgment and for joy. Jesus marches into Jerusalem surrounded by an expectant and ecstatic crowd, but only to weep over the city of peace, which failed to know the very things that make for peace and failed to recognize the coming of her long-awaited king. Jesus accepts the adulation of the crowd, which the Pharisees try to temper, yet weeps over a city and a temple that blindly move toward their inevitable destruction, unable and unwilling to recognize God's revelation in their midst.

The world is being turned upside down. The once-blind Bartimaus sees what others fail to see and perhaps runs with the crowd that hails the coming king, forming part of the voices the religious authorities would silence. Meanwhile Zacchaeus, once alienated by his own greed and corruption, has become a symbol of the true children of Abraham and a friend of the poor. Yet in the heart of the religious establishment, the temple awaits the physical destruction its ethical and spiritual decay has precipitated. Jesus weeps in anguish over a broken and divided city, which is blinder than a roadside beggar and more corrupted by greed than a chief tax collector.

The contrast between the redemptive work of Christ in the lives of Bartimaeus and Zacchaeus and the judgment that still awaits Jerusalem and her temple is terrifyingly stark. They present us with two possibilities. One is so richly infused with redemptive grace that lives are transformed, new relationships are created, and barriers are demolished. A new community emerges in which the poor, the beggar, the blind, the rich, the corrupt, and the greedy find themselves at the same table, their transformed lives centered on the person of Jesus and incorporated into the community of the coming King. The other presents us with the picture of a blind city with coalescing social, political, economic, and religious systems, which in their unrelenting lust for economic gain have become alienated from the very source and origin of all that they seek.

We have then two visions of the city and two versions of urban possibility. If we were to borrow the language of Augustine, we would see in the radically changed fortunes of Bartimaeus and Zacchaeus the hallmarks of the heavenly city, marked by love, justice, and new possibilities of community (Augustine, as cited in D. Smith, 2011). Here the alienated, the excluded, and the marginalized find themselves incorporated in a new, radically inclusive community centered on Jesus. Conversely, in Jesus's lament over Jerusalem and his cleansing of the temple, we see Augustine's earthly city laid bare, marked by corruption and lust for wealth and, having sown the seeds of its own destruction, ultimately doomed.

In his reflections on the Scriptures, Augustine discerned radically different urban forms and urban possibilities. Cities, like the imperial Rome of his day, can be organized to lack love, justice, and community and become a threat to all that might lead to human flourishing. This is the city of gaps, where economic divides deepen, where the fear economy thrives, where people become alienated from one another, and where the poor and the vulnerable are pushed deeper into isolation from the good of the city—Dives (the rich man) and Lazarus on a municipal scale. Yet Augustine reminds us the city is also the place of love, beauty, and holiness, which bring joy to the heart. This is the city, Augustine argues, that Christians are to pine for. This pining is a form of anticipation, a prophetic reimagination of the city surrounding us. Augustine said, "By pining we are already there; we have already cast our hope, like an anchor, on that coast" (Augustine, as cited by D. Smith, 2011, p. 24—26).

A Faithful Reimagining

While in Cape Town, I had the privilege of sitting with a group of Christian leaders from different parts of the city. They reflected the different racial groups that make up this most divided of cities, still grappling with the aftermath of apartheid. We had been exploring the nature of the gaps in the city, how they looked from the perspective of different communities, and how they might be addressed. One of the delegates made a critical observation. He said that we have to understand these gaps are fundamentally a theological problem. He argued that until the church recognizes a divided city is not simply a product of history, an awkward reality we might seek to ameliorate or simply live with, but an issue of fundamental theological concern, we will not move forward. We need a Spirit-inspired pining that grieves over what is, precisely because we know what could be, what should be, and what ultimately in the unfolding of hope, will be. Confronting the gaps begins with a biblically fueled imagination, spilling out onto our streets, which keeps opening up the possibility of what might be in the face of what is.

Around the time we began the Centre for Urban Mission in Nairobi, we were visited by the then Anglican archbishop of Sydney. During the visit, he was taken into Korogocho to visit a small Anglican church in the heart of the informal settlement. As he wandered through the narrow streets, passed the endless rows of tiny iron shacks, carefully navigating the open sewers, he turned to one of those accompanying him and said, "What this place needs is theological education." His guide was momentarily stunned. What this place needs is ... There would be plenty of ways to complete the sentence—entrepreneurs, health professionals, engineers, qualified teachers, development workers ... The list would be endless. But theological educators? Yet the archbishop's comments were prescient, if not prophetic. They very simply and effectively directed us to consider the foundations upon which we believed full and lasting transformation would emerge. What would be the enduring source and basis of hope in this community in their search and longing for a different future?

Of course, so much hangs on what we mean by theology. Theology has been described as the art of answering the questions no one is asking. Dire Straits, in the song "Industrial Disease," scathingly declared, "Philosophy is useless, theology is worse," as if theology is the ultimate exercise in irrelevance. But skepticism about the relevance of theology to daily life is not confined to those outside the church. I suspect that the majority of Christians, on a similar walk round Korogocho, would have been looking for health workers and teachers long before they considered the possibility of theological education.

But what if theology is about casting our anchor on another shore, which is unfolding right here among us? What if theology is about the process of reimagining and anticipating a different today in the light of the revelation of God's tomorrow? What if theology leads us into a life that lives within that possibility, unwilling to conform to the distortions that so easily frame our sense of the normal? When this happens, theology asks us some key questions. It asks us to anticipate right here in our streets, offices, business parks, slums, suburbs, and estates, what the city might look like if it conformed ever more closely to the hallmarks of the reign of God.

This sense of hope, this alternative vision for the future, rooted in God's purposes and intention for his world, is of course central to our understanding of Luke's Gospel. Mary's song celebrates not only what God has done throughout history, but also prophetically anticipates what God will do through the birth of her son. In the inauguration of his ministry in Nazareth, Jesus points to his prophetic fulfillment as the one who will be good news to the poor, open the eyes of the blind, and release captives. His reply to John's question of whether he is the one who is to come points to his fulfillment of this promise. In the sermon on the plain, Jesus points toward a different world, where the poor are the inheritors of the Kingdom of God and those mourning break into mirth. Constantly in the Gospel, we are confronted with the hope of a different kind of future where the poor, the crippled, the blind, and the lame take their seats at the heavenly banquet. Yet this hope is not pushed into some far-distant future beyond the realities of this life. Instead, in the likes of Bartimaeus we see that reality breaking out around Jesus amid those with whom he comes in contact. The future hope is being realized in his presence.

Anticipating Hope

If we are to confront the most profound divisions and yawning gaps within our cities, we will require a faith that is radically open to the possibilities of what God can and will do among us. It will require a faith that gives shape to hope and to the unfolding of new possibilities. Similarly, an essential part of the process of theological reflection is to recognize the shape and meaning of hope in contexts where hope may appear to be in short supply. There are times when we have to grapple with the question of what real hope looks like in a community. Students visiting Kibera would often identify hope as the capacity to leave the community, to move up, to move on, and to move out. No doubt for many young people, their sense of hope would be in a future lived in a different part of the city. But we also need to examine what it means to see a particular place, a concrete reality, in the light of God's future. There is no point pretending this is easy. I cannot count the moments when hope seems so elusive that I cannot capture any sense of possibility beyond the reality that lies before me. This is a challenge that confronts all of us. Yet this eschatological hope, this constant living in anticipation of God's future that is moving towards us, is of the essence of Christian mission.

On one occasion, I was walking through the center of Kibera in the pouring rain. The mud was particularly bad, and my trousers were beginning to look a mess. All along the street in front of me, women sat on wooden stools beneath rather ineffective canopies of plastic sheets hastily rigged up with string. I turned to one woman bravely trying to fry mandazi (similar to doughnuts) on a spluttering fire. "The mud is terrible," I commented, expecting a shared sense of grievance at the weather. "Ah," the woman replied, "rain is a blessing from God." I walked the last short distance to the Centre feeling suitably chastened.

Logic might tell us that people who can move in and out of places such as Kibera or Korogocho, or any of the communities that house the world's one billion slum dwellers, might hold a clearer perspective on hope because their lives are not as bound up in the daily challenges of life. Yet my consistent experience was that my brothers and sisters in Christ within these communities frequently fashioned life with a fabric of hope that was more enduring than my own. If communities need theological education, that education does not need to provide hope, as if hope is a commodity to be supplied by a privileged other. Rather, theological education will require working with people in ways that enable them to frame the hope that is in them.

Resurrection Hope

The final chapter of Luke's Gospel presents us with two of Jesus's disciples walking, dejected, their heads down, away from the very place and moment of the world's redemption. Of course we know Luke's unique account of the events on the Emmaus road leads to a happy ending, but that is not how we first encounter those disciples. David Smith (2007), in his book *Journeying Towards Emmaus*, suggests we must first suspend our knowledge of how the passage concludes if we are to truly empathize with the sense of hopelessness of those two disciples as they "retreat to the countryside, escaping from the scene of the holocaust that has shattered their faith in God and his Messiah and left them facing a future without horizons" (p. 4). In his profound study of the challenges of faith and unfaith in contemporary society, Smith dwells deeply on what are perhaps the most ironic words in the whole of Scripture, "we had hoped." Here, on the third day, Jesus encounters two people whose shattered lives leave them bereft of the very hope that has now been made possible through the resurrection.

I always react negatively to descriptions of people or situations that use the term "hopeless." The word implies a final judgment about the lives of others. Above all, it seems to suggest that any potential for change, hope, and future possibility, lies in the agency of others. Clichéd phrases such as giving hope to the hopeless may be well-meant, but so often they reveal an uncritical appraisal of how relationships are shaped in contexts of need and the paternalism that can form the foundations of helping relationships. Above all, it makes assumptions about where sources of hope are to be found and how they are mediated. None of us possess a surplus of hope to be distributed like cans of beans from a food bank.

Our most fundamental convictions about humanity and the possibilities of God's redemptive purposes leave the word "hopeless" in some sense redundant. It has no place in a lexicon of faith. Yet we cannot hide from the reality that hope for some is at best fleeting, and at worst, a faint memory that life's experience has all but extinguished. Like Lazarus at the rich man's gate, they find themselves without a voice, without agency, and without horizons beyond the perimeters of this life. David Smith helpfully points to the way the Emmaus passage gives us insight into the nature of mission in a world where believers and unbelievers both find themselves struggling with unrealized hopes, expectations, and the existential challenges of a life seemingly devoid of meaning and purpose.

I like to read Luke's Gospel as if the Emmaus road forms a curtain call on the drama of the entire Gospel. Imagine, if you can, the complete cast of Luke's Gospel walking onto the stage together for the final scene on the Emmaus road. In this great denouement, each will find themselves walking alongside Jesus, hidden yet present, challenging them to open their eyes to a world irrevocably changed by the power of the cross and the resurrection. For David Smith, the road is a metaphor for a Western globalized society variously described as post-faith, post-Christian, even post-human. A society that, like Zacchaeus, has found out that unprecedented wealth has resulted in alienation and loss of community and belonging.

If we consider Luke's account of this resurrection appearance of Jesus, we see echoes again of his encounter with Bartimaeus and Zacchaeus. The two marks of his engagement with them, radical inclusion and subversive hospitality, are again in evidence. As we might now expect from Luke, they are revealed in the context of a journey and a meal.

With both Bartimaeus and Zacchaeus, Jesus does what the crowds do not want him not to do. He enters the space of the excluded and invites them to be present with him in ways that will radically reshape their lives and their relationships with his followers and the wider community. While the parable of the rich man and Lazarus could almost be played out as a tableau—there is virtually no movement of the main characters toward each other—the stories of Bartimaeus and Zacchaeus show a converging of lives in the realization of hope. The same is true of the Emmaus road. The two characters present us with the model of the anti-disciple. They are walking away from the resurrection in disbelief and despair. They are the antithesis of a faith community. As such, the risen Christ is an unrecognizable companion on the road who enters the space of their grief and disbelief.

As Jesus encounters the two disciples, we gain a deeper insight into radical inclusion. Jesus is prepared to walk with them and to accompany them in a direction diametrically opposite to the journey they should, and later will, be taking. He draws alongside them in the midst of their disbelief and their abandonment of hope. He provokes them with questions, but these questions emerge from within a shared journey. Interestingly, Luke gives three verses to Jesus's opening of the Scriptures and seven verses to the disciples' account of a resurrection they clearly thought fanciful. A rather generous amount of space is given for a clear declaration of doubt! Yet what seems so evident in the passage is the way the risen Christ brings himself into the company of those who refuse to believe. If Bartimaeus and Zacchaeus remind us that Jesus radically includes in his company those who are rejected and alienated by the religious, economic, and social structures of his day, Cleopas and his friend on the road remind us Jesus will journey with those who cannot see and appear unready to believe the truth of the resurrection. Jesus will walk away from the place of hope in order to accompany those who have no hope.

Of course, this presence in the midst of despair will ultimately prove to be transformational (but we should not forget the miles of walking that led to that point). Jesus's presence with them and his opening of the Scriptures lays the foundation for faith and hope, but the testimony of others and the witness of Scripture seem insufficient for these two disciples. More evidence is needed if their eyes are to be truly opened. We are offered the possibility that Jesus will continue his journey alone, and they will return to their homes, still bereft of hope. Instead, there is the offer of hospitality. Jesus acts as if he will continue his journey, but in response to their urging he accepts their invitation to stay. As with the Zacchaeus story, lives turn around when hospitality is received and a meal is shared. Yet Jesus subverts their hospitality, and its purpose is radically redefined. A meal to console the weary and the doubting becomes the moment of revelation. The separation between Jesus and these erstwhile followers, a separation built on doubt and disbelief and shrouded in despair and grief, is shattered in a moment of thankful breaking of bread. In that moment, the one who was the recipient of hospitality has become the source of it. He breaks and offers the bread and eyes are opened. Their reaction is instant and impulsive. Like Zacchaeus in Luke 19, the disciples' overwhelming impulse is to share with others their newfound sense of gratitude and hope. The experience of salvation puts them immediately back on the road, but in an opposite direction, with a renewed sense of hope and purpose.

Life on the Emmaus Road

It is no coincidence that virtually all the characters we have encountered in Luke's Gospel have been located in some way on the road. Lazarus lies immobile by the roadside, Bartimaeus cries out from it, Zacchaeus struggles to see Jesus on it, and Cleopas and his friend accompany Jesus along it. Meanwhile, the poor, the crippled, the blind, and the lame are to be found in the streets, alleys, roads, and lanes. Bob Ekblad (2005) rightly observes, "In the Gospels Jesus spends most of his time on the road, in fields, on mountains, along the sea, in homes, in forsaken Galilee, incarcerated and on the cross rather than in traditionally holy places like the temple, Jerusalem or the synagogues" (p. 157). When Jesus does frequent religious places, he usually gets in trouble with the religious insiders.

Luke may not have developed the script for a road movie, but roads of one sort or another provide the backdrop for many of his accounts. Jesus is on a journey, and the challenge to us centers on what it means to accompany him and others on it. There are those who would put up barriers to define his travel companions, yet Jesus consistently resists their stance. In so many ways, it seems Jesus is trying to hold together both those who assume themselves to be the natural inheritors of the Kingdom, and favored travelers on the road, and those they would exclude. Ekblad (2005) notes that while Jesus's strong words are never to the sinners, but rather to the religious establishment and the disciples that exclude sinners, Jesus does continually invite religious insiders to join him in extending God's embrace to the excluded other (p. 157). In other words, Jesus is constantly inviting the presumed insider and presumed outsider to form an altogether different community along the road where these divisions are constantly challenged. Moments of conversion seem not to result simply in a changed individual, but also in a new formation of those who accompany him, which challenges the boundaries of belonging. Increasingly, the religious authorities of his day must ask whether they wish to be part of a community that radically incorporates those they would exclude and whether they too will change to make that accommodation.

At the heart of these journeys in community are Emmaus moments that constantly offer the possibility of seeing with new eyes and overflow in actions of praise, generosity, and witness to the risen Christ. Both the religious establishment and the disciples are constantly invited to reorient their lives to see Christ as he really is and accompany him on the road.

This process of a reorientation of faith and a deeper revelation of the Christ among us, from the experience of encountering the excluded, is a kind of Emmaus moment. Father Alex Zanotelli, whom I referred to at the start of this book, tells a story that illustrates that type of encounter clearly:

I remember the story of Jeremias, a giant, working collecting waste material in the dump site (Mukuru). One day he stopped me and said, "Are we like wild beasts that you dare not come to visit us at the dump site?" A punch in the stomach. "Tomorrow I will come to see you." The day after I went to visit Jeremias and his friends in the dumpsite. The people could not believe that a priest would come to visit them! It was an incredible experience for me: an experience of God. "Mission is to sit where people sit," said an experienced missionary, "and let God happen." And he does happen! I remember that on Christmas Day I promised to visit the people of Mukuru in their homes. When I entered the shanty of Jeremias he embraced me with such joy, "Karibu, Alex! Karibu sana!" Then he added, "Alex, please wait for me just a moment. I will be back in a few minutes." And he made me sit on a stone (It was a dilapidated shack without even a stool.). A few minutes later he came back with a loaf of bread in his hands. He broke it before my astonished eyes and said, "Take this, eat it! This is my body broken up for you!" I just felt so ashamed as a Priest (Breaking bread, the Eucharist, is at the heart of our life in Korogocho.). You don't belong to yourself anymore: you are eaten by people. (2002, p. 16).

In this extraordinary moment, which Zanotelli describes so simply and yet so powerfully, we see the way his encounter with Jeremias, a man who made his living scavenging on a municipal dumpsite, challenged his self-identity as a priest and his understanding of the sacraments he administered. His experience suggests a loss of privileged identity and a consuming of self, in order to more deeply identify with Christ and the community he served. Like the disciples on the Emmaus road, his eyes were opened in the breaking of bread.

Without belaboring the point, the story he tells centers on those two experiences of inclusion and hospitality. Again the emphasis falls on the readiness to receive and resisting the impulse to assert ourselves in contexts where we perceive ourselves as the ones with the most to give. Jeremias gave something to Father Alex that Father Alex could never give to him, other than by receiving what was given. Of course, the act is deeply subversive, particularly with anyone who has deep concern for church disciplines and the preservation of distinctions between clergy and lay. But there is a hospitality of grace, freely given and received, which runs through the entire episode.

The power of Father Alex's story lies in his openness to have his faith and identity radically challenged by the faith and agency of Jeremias. The question of who is giving and who is receiving, of where the repositories of truth, wisdom, and revelation of grace lie, suddenly become blurred and confused. Father Alex needs Jeremias in order to discover more fully what it means to be a priest, what it means to celebrate the Eucharist and, perhaps, what it means to be fully human in Christ.

The mission historian Andrew Walls (2002) points to the Ephesian Moment, that is the coming together in the early church of people of two cultures, Jew and Greek. In words that echo our theme of subversive hospitality and radical inclusion, he speaks of how "Two races and two cultures historically separated by the meal table now met at table to share the knowledge of Christ." This coming together, the breaking of the dividing wall of hostility, creates the possibility for both parties to more fully understand what it means to be in Christ. Walls notes, "None of us can reach Christ's completeness on our own. We need each other's vision to correct, enlarge, and focus our own; only together are we complete in Christ" (pp. 78–79).

In Walls's application of the Ephesian Moment to contemporary society, he notes it is of special importance on two accounts— theological and economic. He suggests that for the church to experience its full stature in Christ, it must find true solidarity with a global church that increasingly is made up of those who are poor and marginalized. He poses the question of whether in an age of global Christianity, with the rise of the church in the Global South, the church will be "realized or fractured in this new Ephesian Moment." At the heart of the idea of the Ephesian Moment is a sense that we cannot discover as a church our completeness in Christ without those who are in some sense other than us, and that otherness can be racial, cultural, and economic. Our completeness in Christ rests therefore not simply on a readiness to serve the materially poor but to receive from them, to learn from them, to encounter Christ through them. Henri Nouwen (1986) expresses this very idea when he writes: "I am convinced that one of the greatest missionary tasks is to receive the fruits of the lives of the poor, the oppressed and the suffering as gifts for the salvation of the rich" (p. 48).

Life shared in places of exclusion and marginalization opens the possibility for these avenues of grace; the moments when we see the Gospel in a new light and perhaps see our common humanity for what it really is. The gaps that separate us from each other will constantly deny us that possibility. But how do we become those who accompany Christ on the road in ways that leave us open to these possibilities?

Chapter 13
Finding a New Location

For where your treasure is, there will your heart be also.

--Jesus of Nazareth.

I have tried to capture a sense of what it might mean for churches and individual Christians to draw near to and encounter those at the margins by using the terms radical inclusion and subversive hospitality. These seem to reflect the nature of Jesus's ministry and the encounters he had with others. They illustrate the ways that Jesus enters into and transforms the gaps in his day. Yet to follow Christ in this way we must actively seek out the places where we encounter those who find themselves located at the social and economic margins. It involves a conscious reorientation of our lives toward those at the periphery. Our reasoning for this is essentially missional in that it reflects a desire to see our lives patterned on the mission of God, revealed in the life and ministry of Jesus. It is rooted in the desire actively to follow Christ in the places of his leading. It is for this reason that Costas (1989) argued, as we saw earlier, that the base of evangelism is an association with the lowest level, the most poor and marginalized in society (p. 62).

For some this has meant a literal relocation, a conscious decision to move into a place of poverty or marginalization. The writer and Christian anarchist Dave Andrews describes the experience of Jim Dowling and Anne Rampa who, inspired by the Christian worker movement, sought to live out this relocation within their native Australia. They describe their experience as follows: "We set out not just to serve the poor, but to live with the poor, and indeed to try to become poor by turning our backs on the seductions of our materialist society, and striving for a life of voluntary poverty" (as cited by Andrews, 1999, p. 104).

There is always the danger that this type of approach will be seen as a kind of hard core Christianity to be taken up by a very select few whose specific sense of calling leads them in this direction. There is undeniably something distinctive about the vocation of those who sense God's leading to live among those at the very margins of society. Many of us may not discern that specific calling. However, our common vocation to follow Christ will inevitably lead all of us into a tension with values that are bound up in consumerism and into a reorientating of life toward an identification with the poor and marginalized. S.T. Kimbrough (2013), reflecting on the enduring relevance of the legacy of Charles Wesley's thinking, notes that if we follow Wesley's lead, working for the poor, and here we might rephrase that to working in solidarity with the poor, becomes integral to the exercise of our vocations and daily lives (p. 90). How then do we live out this vocation?

There is much being written about those who make the decision to move across the globe in order to share the life of people at the margins. Accounts of movements, such as those termed the New Friars, describe the lived-out vocation of those who commit themselves, in different ways, to share in the lives of the poor (Bessenecker, 2006). Such movements are a vital corrective to many expressions of Western mission that have comfortably distanced themselves from the realities of the life of those at the economic margins. They reveal a desire for more authentic, incarnational models of mission that do not seek to isolate themselves from those who live at the margins of global cities in the majority world. However, my unease with such movements, or at least the narratives that surround them, is that they frequently fail to describe the agency of the communities they enter and serve. For instance, the majority of the members of the New Friars appear largely young, white, and college-educated.

What then are the other narratives that might need to be told? During my time working at the Centre for Urban Mission, some of the people who created the deepest impression on me were Kenyan Christians who had made the decision to locate themselves within the city's slums and informal settlements. For some, the decision to live in the slum had never been a matter of choice. Like many of Nairobi's migrants, this was the place where they landed when they entered the city. Staying in the slums began as an economic necessity, but staying, once their economies improved, became a matter of conviction. One such person was Barrack who worked with us both at the Centre and in St. Jerome Parish. I asked him about his reasons for entering and remaining in Kibera. He said:

> Like most city migrants who find it easier to begin life in Kibera (or any other informal settlement), I moved in with one of my cousins. My intention was to stay temporarily as I sought a gainful employment before moving out to a better estate. However, with time I developed a relationship with the people in Kibera, initially in a local Anglican church of St. Jerome and later with the community. I found people who seem to care about one another in the ups and downs of life. As a result, I found a deeper sense of belonging to the community. I no longer saw myself as a sojourner but rather part and parcel of the community. The urge to leave was no longer there, and instead it was replaced by the joy of living in Kibera. I made this decision to stay in Kibera as a single young man in 2002 and 2003. However, when I married in 2006, things did not change. This is because while we were courting we discussed a lot about living in Kibera. We were both in agreement that we will continue living in Kibera.
>
> As a family we have continued to enjoy the strong community bond experienced in Kibera with a strong social capital. Our lives are so open to the people we

interact with. People visit us any time with or without any appointment, and we too do likewise. The family has had to face the reality of living in a deprived community like Kibera with very limited service provision by the local authority. We have had to live the hard way just like other members of the community do. My children have not had the comfort of recreational places or uninterrupted electricity. Sometimes we fall victim to those practising extortion in the community.

Living in this community helped me to discover my calling. I came to have a first-hand experience of ministry to the marginalised, as one of the marginalised, at least by choice. I have learnt and continue to learn what it means to minister to a hungry, jobless, sick and oppressed person, who is both body and soul, in a community within a divided city.

Many see my remaining in Kibera as a failure to progress in life. We live in a time that values prosperity and upward mobility, and where you live is a sign of that. Whenever we host visitors (both local and international) in the community, the question of how long we have lived in Kibera or how long we intend to stay often comes up. My response has always been the same. "I am comfortable where I am because my ministry calling is to the people we live with here in Kibera."

I am aware that material possession as well as a high standard of living is a good thing. However, they are not the only things that matter in life. Values and character shaped by faith in Christ are stronger indicators of success. I would like to see that happen in the lives of the people we live with on a regular basis. My motivation to stay is to see this growth happening in people's lives as we interact regularly, not just when I am out there doing mission."

Barrack and his family have moved up within Kibera, but they remain within its wider community. What strikes me in his reflection is the sense, as with Father Zanotelli, that the margins can be places of gift and learning. There is a clear sense of cost that he and his family bear, but also a sense of joy, privilege, and belonging. These are in some sense the hallmarks of the redemptive spaces Jesus creates within the gaps. He is present in ways that defy boundaries and lead to joy and celebration. Saying this is not to airbrush out the deep personal cost, but to acknowledge that those who cross the divided city often acknowledge that they find themselves in places where the experience may be as much gift, grace, and finding purpose as it is of loss.

While for Barrack the decision to enter Kibera was not one of choice, for others it quite clearly is. Imbumi Makuku is a pastor in the Reformed Presbyterian Church. He currently pastors a church in Kibera but earlier in his ministry he made the decision to move into Mukuru Kayaba, a slum in Nairobi's industrial area, in order to plant a church there. He lived for two years in the community and continued to pastor there for an additional six years. It was an experience that continues to shape his ministry in Kibera. Yet it was a decision few around him understood at the time. He said:

> The decision to move into Mukuru Kayaba was not understood well by colleagues who thought I was throwing away a good education ... which fitted me most for a middle-class church. Others thought I was escaping from mainstream church life. The common thread was that I did not know God's will for my life. What I learnt at an early age as a believer was that there was no need to continue justifying my ministry calling but that God in his own time would vindicate the work. The mixed reactions continue to this day as elitist and middle-class pastors that I interact with look at the work as inferior. My major encouragement has been from those who have been brought up in poverty and understand the power of the Gospel to bring about true transformation.

This experience of not being understood is no doubt repeated in the lives of many and in some ways echoes the very accusations leveled against Jesus for the company he chose to keep. Sometimes the cost of relocation to the margins comes from the attitudes of those who fail to comprehend the impulse of the Gospel that leads us there. Yet relocation is at some level the call to all of us. The margins in Luke's Gospel are not simply a physical or economic space. Spatial and economic divides reveal a deeper alienation in relationships and a narrowing of worlds. Our starting point will need to be at the level of our attitudes, perspectives, and relationships. We may need to change the way we see the world.

A Relocation of the Heart

In the industrial area of Nairobi, just down the road from the college where I worked, is an estate that goes by the name Shauri Moyo. It is an area of high-density and low-cost city council housing. The name is not easily translatable into English but one possibility would be "an affair of the heart." It was there, among members of an African Independent Church, the Holy Spirit Church of East Africa, where I first encountered a community of believers made up almost entirely of those living at the social, economic, and in many respects, religious margins of the city. I had barely been in Kenya for a month, and yet this was for me the beginning of a form of conversion. It was the beginning of a reshaping of my understanding, a glimpse of the world from the perspective of a part of the body of Christ whose expressions of faith and experience of life appeared so contrary to my own.

As worshipers in turbans and white robes gathered from across the city and danced and sang, shouted, listened, and prayed, I was initially most aware of the distance between us. The gaps of language and culture seemed immense. This was church as I had never known it before. Yet in the midst of such difference, there was also the sense of that which drew us toward each other. In our different ways, we were each hungry, thirsty, empty, longing to glimpse that which faith alone makes possible. One reason that members of African Independent churches wear robes is because it acts as a leveler. The shapeless kanzu covers distinctions of wealth and status that might otherwise create false division. Meanwhile shoes, often a signifier of wealth, are left outside the door of this iron-sheet holy place.

In the opening chapter of this book, I referred to Charles Elliott's description of the two jaws of guilt and perceptions of powerlessness that stifle our abilities to engage with the gaps, the deep fissures of inequality and disparity that increasingly define the global economy. I suspect that navigating an alternative response begins with an affair of the heart, a relocation in our sense of belonging and identity. We need to rediscover Christ in ways that bring us into solidarity with those at the margins. This involves a realigning of our perspective, a movement of heart and mind that consciously seeks to see the world and experience faith by standing in another's shoes. The Argentinian Liberation Theologian Jose Miguez Bonino (1980) grappled with this challenge, asking of himself where his sense of commitment, loyalty, and perspective were really found. Ultimately he found no via media, no comfortable middle ground. Bonino writes:

> There is no socially and politically neutral theology; in the struggle for life and against death, theology must take sides. I have to ask myself, What is my social location as theologian? Whose interests and concerns am I serving? Whose perspective on reality, whose experience am I adopting? And, since it is a conflict, against whom—temporarily and conditionally, but no less resolutely—am I struggling? (pp. 1154–1158)

Looking at the parable of the rich man and Lazarus, it is as if Bonino is inviting us to examine ourselves and see what posture we adopt within the narrative, on which side of the gap we appear to be located, whether it is the table or the gate that shapes our attitudes, values, and concerns. Yet we have seen that while Jesus of Nazareth locates himself among the marginalized, at the periphery, he does so in ways that create new redemptive spaces no longer defined by barriers of indifference, alienation, and exclusion. In these redemptive spaces,

Bartimaus has the voice and agency that Lazarus never found, while Zacchaeus discovers what the rich man never knew, the privilege of being a true child of Abraham.

Our vocation in a divided world is to recover these redemptive spaces. One way we do this is through a process of remembering, through finding identity in shared memory. Mary's song in the first chapter of Luke is precisely this. She remembers the merciful actions of a God in history in ways that anticipate the Christ who will raise up the poor and scatter the rich, proud, and the powerful. This subversive memory becomes the song of a new community whose members find their shared identity in their identification with Christ. We too must recover that subversive memory, for it is as we remember Christ that we re-member the church. It is then that we identify with and long for that community that embraces the excluded, heals the broken, and models itself on the one who was rich yet for our sake became poor.

Conclusion
Where Lazarus is Poor No Longer

David Runcorn (2003) says of the persons of the Trinity, "They live and know each other in the simple ecstasy of giving" (p. 7). The Trinity is the model of our life together and that ecstasy of giving, that joyful generosity of spirit, is of the very essence of Christian community. Yet so often our experience of church, of faith, of community bears so little resemblance to that which we are called to be.

One of the things we most miss from our sabbatical in South Africa is the weekly cycle of a Thursday evening community meal. It was a far from ideal arrangement, and the church that ran it was deeply aware of its imperfections. It continually faced the struggle to retain a vision for creating authentic community, while resisting the drift toward running yet another feeding program for some of Cape Town's street dwellers. Yet for all its problems, there were hints of Emmaus road moments. Seated at shared tables, around plates of rice and chicken, stories were told, tears shed, songs sung, prayers spoken and unspoken. A different kind of space seemed possible where Lazarus spoke, where a divided city met, ate and drank in the company of each other. This was not the just city, far from it. This was not even the redemptive space where barriers are overcome. But it provided what all of us need, what we each must discover, a space to fire the imagination, to find a different perspective rooted in the other—a place to meet, to listen, to hear.

I began this book with the story of a beggar at my gate who prayed that God would touch the heart of his more privileged brother. At the time, I heard that prayer as something manipulative and insincere, and perhaps it was. But in my journey through Luke's Gospel, I find myself conceding that this man's prayer identified my need at least as much as it articulated his. I might wish God had chosen a different approach, and I certainly would have preferred an altogether different messenger, but the prayer for a generous heart is not one we can dismiss lightly.

The account of the beggar at my gate tells a broken story. Like Jesus's parable of the rich man and Lazarus, it is a story that doesn't end well. It is also a story told from only one side of the gate, from one perspective. There is no simple or elegant solution that would have resolved the differences and tensions between our two worlds. But had I been more sensitive to the workings of grace, more attentive to the promptings of the Spirit, there was in that encounter the possibility of finding an alternative, redemptive space that would have made a difference in both our lives.

It is Sunday morning, and I am treading a very familiar path toward St. Jerome Church in Kibera. Along the way, I hear a voice call my name. I know what will be coming next. A young lad with learning difficulties grabs me by the hand. The conversation begins. It is the same one we have pretty much every week and usually ends with a request that I take him to America when I return (I have given up insisting that I am English). The women by the roadside laugh and call out his name. He is known to everyone in this part of Kibera. He has a tough home life, and my attempts to get him into school have been unfruitful. I fear for his future, but I know that in this place, which is warned against in almost every U.K. and U.S. travel advisory, he is at home. He is different, but known, and somehow seems to have his place in the community. He may drop into the church at some point in the morning. He won't stay throughout the service and seems to have his own set of rules of when to sit or stand or speak, but that is okay. We seem to be pretty good at adapting to whoever is there. And of course, I should know. If anyone stands out in this congregation or doesn't quite fit in, it's me!

Later in the service, we may celebrate communion. It is those moments when I sense the deepest privilege of being included among people to whom, in every other sphere of life, I could not belong. It is Christ who brings us together in this feast. The feast, celebrated beneath an iron-sheet roof, is meager. It is a morsel, a sip, but also a wondrous foretaste and promise of something beyond our wildest imagining. Yet it asks so much more of me than I have felt able to give. Around this table, I have sensed that I live too much of my life peering into the gaps and moving only tentatively within them. I have become aware of my inclination to retreat from the chaos, uncertainty, and vulnerability that they represent. But from within these gaps there are other voices to be heard at the gate.

Bartimaeus shouts from the roadside, and at times I wish he would be quieter. He sees so much in Jesus that I have not grasped and endlessly unsettles my sense of what it means to follow him. Zacchaeus is also there. He is rejoicing in the liberating richness of a life marked by justice, generosity, and sacrifice. I want to urge a more cautious following, but I know he will have none of it. For it is in the places where these voices are heard, echoing through the gaps, redeeming the silence, that another sound emerges. Finally Lazarus, poor no longer, reaches out across the chasm and extends the invitation of the one who was rich but for our sake became poor.

> *Come to the feast,*
> *There is room at the table.*
> *Come let us meet in this place.*
> *With the King of all kindness*
> *Who welcomes us in,*
> *With the wonder of love,*
> *And the power of grace.*
> Stuart Townend, "Vagabonds"

References

Andrews, D. (1999). *Christi-Anarchy: Discovering a radical spirituality of compassion.* Eugene, OR: Wipf and Stock.

Arbuckle, G. (2010). *Culture, inculturation and theologians: A postmodern critique.* Collegeville, MN: Liturgical Press.

Bailey K. (2008). The New Testament Job: The parable of Lazarus and the rich man, an exercise in Middle Eastern New Testament studies. *Theological Review, 29.* 12–30.

Bell, R. (2012). *Love wins: At the heart of life's big questions.* London: Harper Collins.

Bessenecker, S. (2006). *The new friars: The emerging movement serving the world's poor.* Downers Grove, IL: InterVarsity Press.

Bock, D. (1996). *Luke 9:51–24:53 Baker exegetical commentary on the New Testament.* Grand Rapids, MI: Baker Books.

Bonino, M. (1980). For life against death. *Christian Century.* 1154–1158.

Butler, C. (2014). *Henri Lefebvre: Spatial politics, everyday life and the right to the city.* Abingdon, UK: Routledge Cavendish Publishing.

Capon, R. (1988). *The parables of grace.* Grand Rapids, MI: William B. Eerdmans Publishing Company.

Caputo, J. The insistence of God: A theology of perhaps. http://www.jrdkirk.com/2013/10/02/john-caputo-insistence-hospitality

Card, M. (2011). *Luke: The gospel of amazement.* Downers Grove, IL: InterVarsity Press.

Castells, M. (2000). *The information age: Economy society and culture. Volume III End of millennium* (2nd ed.). Oxford, UK: Blackwell Publishing.

Chambers, R. (1997). *Whose reality counts? Putting the last first.* London: ITDG Publishing.

Claiborne, S. (2006) *The irresistible revolution: Living as an ordinary radical.* Grand Rapids, MI: Zondervan.

Coetzee, J.M. (1983). *The life and times of Michael K.* London: Vintage Books.

Costas, O. (1989). *Liberating news: A theology of contextual evangelization.* Grand Rapids, MI: William B. Eerdmans Publishing Company.

Craddock, F. (1990). *Luke. Interpretation: A Bible commentary for teaching and preaching.* Louisville, KY: John Knox Press.

Dafe, F. (2009). No business like slum business? The political economy of the continued existence of slums: A case study of Nairobi. *London School of Economics Development Working Paper*, series number 9–98.

Davis, M. (1992). *City of quartz: Excavating the future in Los Angeles.* New York: Vintage Publishing.

Davey, A. (2002). *Urban Christianity and the global order: Theological resources for an urban future.* London: SPCK Publishing.

Ekblad, A.R. (2005). *Reading the Bible with the damned.* Louisville, KY: Westminster John Knox Press.

Elate, S. S. (2004). African urban history in the future. In Faola, T. & Salm, S. (Eds.), *Globalization and urbanization in Africa.* Asmara, Eritrea: Africa World Press.

Eliot, T.S. (1961). *Selected poems.* London: Faber.

Elliott, C. (1985). *Praying the Kingdom: Towards a political spirituality.* London: Darton, Longman and Todd.

Fabella V. & Torres, S. (Eds.). (1984). *Irruption of the Third World: Challenge to theology.* New York: Orbis Books.

Fainstein, S. (2010). *The just city.* New York: Cornell University Press.

Falola, T. & Salm, S. (Eds.). (2004). *Globalization and urbanization in Africa.* Asmara, Eritrea: Africa World Press.

Foster, R. (1981). *Freedom and simplicity.* London: SPCK/Triangle.

Freyne, S. (2004). *Jesus a Jewish Galilean: A new reading of the Jesus story.* London: T and T Clark International.

Githogo, J. (2006). African hospitality: Is it compatible with the ideal of Christ's hospitality? *The Churchman*, 120(2).

Green, J. (1997). *The Gospel of Luke.* Grand Rapids, MI: William B. Eerdmans Publishing Company.

Hake, A. (1997). *African metropolis: Nairobi's self-help city.* London: Palgrave Macmillan.

Harries, J. (2012). *Vulnerable mission: Insights into Christian mission to Africa from a position of vulnerability.* Pasadena, CA: William Carey Library Publishers.

Heuertz, C. & Pohl, C. (2010). *Friendship at the margins: Discovering mutuality in service and mission.* Downers Grove, IL: InterVarsity Press.

Hollis, L. (2013). *Cities are good for you: The genius of the metropolis.* London: Bloomsbury.

Horsley, R. (Ed.). (2008). *In the shadow of empire: Reclaiming the Bible as a history of faithful resistance.* Louisville, KY: Westminster John Knox Press.

Horsley, R. (2009). *Covenant economics: A biblical vision of justice for all.* Louisville, KY: Westminster John Knox Press.

Jeffrey, D.L. (2012). *Luke.* Grand Rapids, MI: Brazos Press.

Jeremias, J. (1972). *The parables of Jesus* (3rd ed.). London: SCM.

Katongole, E. (2011). *The sacrifice of Africa: A political theology for Africa.* Cambridge, UK: William B. Eerdmans Publishing Company.

Kimbrough, S. (2013). *Radical grace: Justice for the poor and marginalized —Charles Wesley's views for the twenty-first century.* Eugene, OR: Cascade Books.

Kuhn, K. (2010). *Luke: The elite evangelist.* Collegeville, MN: Liturgical Press.

Linthicum, R. (2005). *Building a people of power.* Franklin, TN: Authentic Books.

Longenecker, R. (Ed.). (2000). *The challenge of Jesus' parables.* Grand Rapids, MI: William B. Eerdmans Publishing Company.

Lupton, R. (2012). *Toxic charity: How churches and charities hurt those they help (and how to reverse it).* New York: HarperOne.

Moore, M. (2011). *Wealth watch: A study of socio-economic conflict in the Bible.* Eugene, OR: Pickwick Publications.

Morgan, S., Ismalia, Z., & Salisu, A. (2010). Patron-client relationships and low education among youth in Kano, Nigeria. In *African Studies Review, 53*(1), 79–103.

Morris, L. (1974). *Luke: An introduction and commentary.* Leicester, UK: InterVarsity Press.

Moyo, D. (2010). *Dead aid: Why aid is not working and how there is another way for Africa.* London: Penguin.

Murray, M. & Myers, G. (Eds.). (2006). *Cities in contemporary Africa.* New York: Palgrave Macmillan.

Moxnes, H. (1988). *The economy of the Kingdom: Social conflict and economic relations in Luke's Gospel.* Philadelphia, PA: Fortress Press.

Moxnes, H. (1991). Patron-client relations and the new community. In Neyrey, J. (Ed.). *The social world of Luke–Acts: Models of interpretation.* Peabody, MA: Hendrickson Publishers.

Myers, B. (1999). *Walking with the poor.* New York: Orbis Books.

Myers, C. (2008). *Binding the strong man: A political reading of Mark's story of Jesus (20th anniversary ed.).* New York: Orbis Books.

Myers, G. (2011). *African cities: Alternative visions of urban theory and practice.* London: Zed Books.

Neyrey, J. (Ed.). (1991). *The social world of Luke–Acts: Models for interpretation.* Peabody, MA: Hendrickson Publishers.

Nouwen, H. (1986). *In the house of the Lord.* London: Darton, Longman and Todd.

Nouwen, H. (1986). *Reaching out: The three movements of the spiritual life.* London: Fount.

Obudho, R. (1997). Nairobi: National capital and regional hub. In Rakodi, C. (Ed.) *The urban challenge in Africa: Growth and management of its large cities.* New York: United Nations University Press.

Parsons, A. (2010). *The seven myths of slums: Challenging popular prejudices about the world's urban poor.* London: Share the World's Resources.

Patella, M. (2005). *The Gospel according to Luke.* Collegeville, MN: Liturgical Press.

Paton, A. (2003). *Cry, the beloved country.* New York: Scribner Publishing.

Piketty, T. (2014). *Capital in the twenty-first century.* Cambridge, MA: Harvard University Press.

Randerson, James. *Guardian Newspaper.* December 6, 2006 .http://www.theguardian.com/money/2006/dec/06/business.internationalnews .

Runcorn, D. (2003). *Choice, desire and the will of God: What more do you want?* London: SPCK Publishing.

Sassen, S. (1999). *Globalization and its discontents.* New York: The New Press.

Saunders, D. (2011). *Arrival city.* London: Windmill Books.

Schweizer, (1984). *The Good News according to Luke.* Atlanta, GA: John Knox Press.

Selby, P. (1991). *Belonging: Challenge to a tribal church.* London: SPCK Publishing.

Sennett, R. (1990). *Conscience of the eye: The design and social life of cities.* London: Faber.

Simone, A. (2005). *Urban Africa: Changing contours of survival in the city.* Dakar, Senegal: CODESRIA Books.

Simone, A. (2004). *For the city yet to come: Changing African life in four cities.* Durham, NC: Duke University Press.

Smith, C. (2011). Urban pessimism and a Gospel of hope. In *Journal of Urban Mission.* http://jofum.com/editorial/articles/urban-pessimism-and-the-gospel-of-hope.

Smith, D. (2007). *Moving towards Emmaus: Hope in a time of uncertainty.* London: SPCK Publishing.

Smith, D. (2011). *Seeking a city with foundations: Theology for an urban world.* Leicester, UK: InterVarsity Press.

Sobrino, J. (1978). *Christology at the crossroads.* New York: Orbis Books.

Soja, E. (2010). *Seeking spatial justice.* Minneapolis, MN: University of Minnesota Press.

South African Catholic Bishops' Conference Parliamentary Liaison Office. The private security industry. Briefing Paper 313, December 2012.

Stiglitz, J. (2013). *The price of inequality.* London: Penguin Books.

Talbert, C. (1984). *Reading Luke: A literary and theological commentary on the third Gospel.* New York: Crossroad.Publishing.

Tokunboh, A. (2006). *The Africa Bible commentary.* Nairobi, Kenya: Word Alive Publishers.

Walls, A. (2002). *The cross-cultural process in Christian history.* New York: Orbis Books.

Wright, N.T. (2004). *Luke for everyone.* Louisville, KY: Westminster John Knox Press.

Wright, S. (2000). Parables on poverty and riches. Longenecker, R. (Ed.). *The challenge of Jesus's parables.* Grand Rapids, MI: William B. Eerdmans Publishing Company.

Yancey, P. (1997). *What's so amazing about grace?* Grand Rapids, MI: Zondervan.

Zanotelli, A. (2002). A grace freely given. In Pierli, F. & Abeledo, Y. (Eds.). *Slums: The challenge of evangelization.* Nairobi, Kenya: Paulines Publications Africa. 13–17.

About the Author

Colin Smith is Dean of Mission Education at the Church Mission Society (CMS) in Oxford. He spent 10 years in parish ministry in inner London and then fourteen years serving with CMS in Nairobi, Kenya. Whilst in Nairobi, he was Director of the Centre for Urban Mission and on the staff of Carlile College and St Paul's University.

About ULP

Urban Loft Publishers focuses on ideas, topics, themes, and conversations about all things urban. Renewing the city is the central theme and focus of what we publish. It is our intention to blend urban ministry, theology, urban planning, architecture, urbanism, stories, and the social sciences, as ways to drive the conversation. While we lean towards scholarly and academic works, we explore the fun and lighter sides of cities as well. We publish a wide variety of urban perspectives, from books by the experts about the city to personal stories and personal accounts of urbanites who live in the city.

www.urbanloftpublishers.com
@the_urban_loft

.

www.ingramcontent.com/pod-product-compliance
Lightning Source LLC
LaVergne TN
LVHW051234080426

835513LV00016B/1584